The Gift Bearers

The Gift Bearers
A Sculptural Interpretation
of Christmas Traditions Through the Centuries
©1994 Brenda G. Morris

Brenmor Books
P. O. Box 618
Midlothian, VA 23113

Library of Congress Catalog Number: 94-96636

ISBN 0-9643930-0-X

The Gift Bearers

Sculptures, Text, and Book Design
by Brenda Goin Morris

Editor: Lynne B. Robertson

Photographer: Jeff S. Saxman

Acknowledgements

I would like to genuinely thank my family, friends, and all those whom I have relied upon for help or professional advice throughout this project: *Patty Pryor,* whose suggestion initiated my first Victorian figure; *Lynne Mooney,* for sharing her knowledge in doll construction and working with clay; my *Mom, mother-in-law,* and *Aunt Marie,* for donating mink collars, fabrics, antique jewelry, and trims for the costumes; *Sammi Nielsen* for her encouragement and support; *Lou Montgomery,* a great "PR" person who has taken every occasion to promote the sculptures and the book; and *the Valentine Museum* and *the Make-A-Wish Foundation,* for the opportunity to display my Christmas figures to the Richmond community.

In addition, thanks are extended to *Frank Kostek,* a gifted artist whose counsel at the onset of this project was greatly appreciated; *Bill Nelson,* well-known graphics artist and doll maker, who shared information concerning book publishing and doll-making, inspiring me to remake all the figures; *Payson Jones III,* for sharing his synopsis of "The Other Wise Man"; and *Anita Rose,* artist and neighbor, for putting me in contact with just the right people.

I am also very grateful to *Cecilia Donohue* for reviewing the manuscript for religious and historical accuracy; my good friend, *Nancy Payne,* who proofread the text several times and made the dolls a tourist attraction for her out-of-town guests; *Susan Reid,* a talented art director and long-time friend, who lent her expertise to the design of the book; *Jane Lohr,* creative artist and special friend, for her professional advice and help with the photography; and *Cosby-Bowyer Inc.* for assistance in this endeavor.

Special thanks are given to *Jeff Saxman,* a very talented young man with a bright future, who has spent endless hours making sure each figure was perfectly photographed; and *Lynne Robertson,* who has been more than an editor. Because of my numerous revisions, she has had to read this manuscript many times. Lynne's rewrites have given a special warmth to my endless pages of facts, and through her example, I have learned much. Both Lynne and Jeff share my love of this project and are equally excited to see the book in print.

To the people of *Mobility, Inc.,* I owe a special thanks for bringing all the pieces together to create a quality book.

Lastly, thanks are given to my children, *Matt and Jennifer,* for patience and understanding with the hours I've spent at the drawing board and computer, in the workshop, or buried in stacks of research books; and my husband, *Dale,* who has read and corrected many revisions of this book and has been supportive of my project since its conception.

To Jennifer and Matthew

Contents

❧ The Christmas Sculptures

ntroduction

The world's most festive, spiritual, and colorful customs of Christmas are like threads in a tapestry, woven in and out over time. Through the centuries, customs have varied, and the names of special celebrations have changed. Yet three main threads have held this tapestry together as each region of the world added its own rich textures and subtle shadings to the celebration of the holiday season. Consequently, we have inherited an illustrious canvas of traditions for all to enjoy.

Those threads which have remained constant since earliest recorded times are the legends and folktales referring to a magical gift bearer; the mid-winter celebrations honoring the old and bringing in the new; and the belief in a Supreme Being, whether one God or many gods and goddesses. Of these three main threads, the one holding the most profound significance for children throughout time has been the gift bearer.

This magical figure has assumed many forms over the centuries. Legends and customs developed the specialness of different personages who gave gifts as well as those who handed out reprimands. Many of these characters and customs were associated with the primitive year-end celebrations of Saturnalia, the Calends, and Yuletide that balanced fall harvesting with spring planting, dark lingering nights with short gray days, and life sparring with death. Religious beliefs ranged from the Roman's family of gods and the Germanic people's All-Father god to the Christian's worship of one God, His Son, and the Holy Spirit.

St. Nicholas

From its beginning, Christianity took these main threads from the early history of mankind and began weaving them into a lasting, cherished Christmas season. Ancient wanderings, turmoil, and discoveries contributed to the mid-winter holiday pattern. Settlers in the New World revived Old World customs fragmented by the changes which occurred during the Protestant Reformation. Americans assimilated the Christmas customs and traditions of European ancestors into their new lives here. In the process, holiday practices typical only to America were woven into this centuries-old tapestry. An unusually beautiful season was created for us to enjoy today; a memorable time when feelings of joy, warmth, and happiness fill the air, and a spirit of kindness is exhibited toward all men no matter what their differences.

Within the Christmas cloth were woven the beloved, age-old symbols of universal love — the gift bearers. They were those unique representatives of joy, peace, and hope who forever brought mankind together once a year. These benevolent figures and their relationship to history held a special fascination for artist Brenda Goin Morris. Desiring a clearer understanding of gift-giving customs, Brenda read volumes of books for information relating to Christmas. Her extensive research revealed a world of history, cultures, period costumes, time lines, legends, fairy tales, and an abundance of magical figures who brought gifts to children or who had added a cherished tradition to the Christmas

Santa Claus

season. Each figure demanded to come to life under her skillful, artistic hands.

Springing from the Christmas celebrations that signified the deeper spiritual qualities of God and man were born sculptures representing the gift-giving Magi, angels, and saints. Her collection of wonderfully charming, realistic Christmas characters, from ancient to 19th century gift bearers, also includes Europe's St. Nicholas, various American Santas, and lesser known figures from folklore such as the Viking Odin, the hearth goddess Berchta, the kind, witch-like Italian Befana, and Russia's tireless Baboushka. Each one artistically personifies a facet of the gift-giving tradition. Different cultures, countries, dress, and time periods are seen in each of these special doll sculptures.

Aside from the historical significance of individual characters, each gift bearer's face was meticulously sculpted and its body carefully assembled. Their costumes were individually designed and sewn from unique fabrics, leathers, and furs — some new, some old, some antique. Color selections, textures, and fine details received careful attention. Many of the accessories were crafted, hand carved, or collected with a specific character in mind.

This book represents the culmination of Brenda's creative talents and historic research. All thirty-seven sculptures in her personal collection, so beautifully photographed by Jeff Saxman,

illustrate the labor of love given to each character. To fully appreciate the complexity of these figures, the reader must understand something of early civilizations — their histories, religious beliefs, and ceremonies — as well as the development of Christianity and the thought behind its celebrations. Each legendary figure takes you on a magical journey into the holiday celebrations of times past. The customs give the characters life and purpose. Accompanied by historical background, they evolve into their reason for being. One by one, each character will step from the pages into the warmth of your home.

The Gift Bearers is an informative, delightful, and endearing mixture of history and folklore surrounding the Christmas season. It is the artist's gift to each of you.

Lynne B. Robertson

The Ancient of Days

As we rush about in the days preceding Christmas, do we ever stop to wonder how our many delightful holiday traditions began? The Biblical account of the birth of Jesus, when the Magi presented the precious gifts of gold, frankincense, and myrrh, is considered the first Christmas. But what about the festive spirit of the season, the gathering of family and friends, the bountiful tables overflowing with traditional holiday dishes, and the fragrant scents of evergreens filling the air? The traditions of the yule log, holly, mistletoe, carolers, and Santas must have an origin too. And what about everyone's favorite tradition - - the giving of gifts? How did Nicholas, the Bishop of Myra evolve into Santa Claus? Are gift-giving practices and other Christmas customs derived from Christian heritage, or could they possibly predate the birth of Jesus? Did the superstitious pagan world with its carousing spirit have any influence in what we recognize today as the holiday season?

To find the answers to these questions, we must unravel an extraordinary tapestry of Christmas customs and traditions, which has been in a weaving process for almost two thousand years. The myriad of twisted threads lead to the "ancient of days" where we find men battling each other, developing cultures, sharing customs, and forming civilizations. Our story begins here as we trace the threads of lively traditions surrounding ancient celebrations to the years when the golden strands of Christian beliefs were added.

Earliest man relied on nature for his livelihood, holding both fear and wonderment for a host of unexplained forces as he struggled to survive. He worshipped the numerous elements of nature and assigned to each phenomenon a "god" who was properly appeased in due season. The long stretch of gloomy winter months held special significance for these primitive people who regarded the sun as the omnipotent giver of life and associated the darkness of the season with evil.

The shortest day of the year was called the winter solstice. During the seemingly endless nights of the solstice season, magic acts and religious ceremonies meant to revive the fading sun were performed. The somber prayers and rituals were followed by a time of festive celebration welcoming in the new year. Although these ceremonies varied in dates and customs from region to region, people everywhere celebrated the mid-winter season with a universal purpose, to save the sun.

Appeasement of the gods continued to be the main thread of pagan worship throughout ancient times. Rituals expanded and myths were created to support beliefs in powers beyond man's control. Each civilization from the Egyptian to the Roman absorbed and built upon the customs of the previous one as people intermingled through the centuries. While diverse religions evolved, with all the trappings of their seasonal festivals and customs, the stage was being set for a more spiritual form of worship.

*T*he Magi were the first gift bearers associated with the birth of Jesus. Through interpretation of the stars and planets, the Magi discerned an important event was to occur, the birth of a great King. They followed a bright star in the sky to Bethlehem, arriving twelve days after the birth of Jesus.

Tradition has appointed three Magi, or Wise Men, because there are three gifts mentioned in the Bible. According to a 6th century Armenian legend, three kings gave the symbolic gifts to the Holy Infant. Melchior, the long-bearded old king of Arabia, gave a coffer of gold in tribute. King Balthazar of Ethiopia offered frankincense as a sign of His divinity; and Gaspar, the young King of Tarsus, bestowed myrrh, a symbol of the crucifixion. In the Christian world today, January 6, the twelfth day after Christmas, is known as Epiphany (Manifestation) or Three Kings Day.

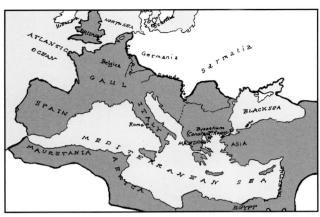

At the height of Rome's rule in 117 A.D., the vast Roman Empire (shown in gray) extended all the way around the Mediterranean Sea. The Rhine and Danube rivers provided a natural boundary between the civilized Romans and the warring Germanic tribes to the north. By the 4th century, the Empire was divided into Eastern and Western regions as shown by the dotted line.

In the century before the birth of Christ, the Romans ruled a vast Empire extending around the Mediterranean Sea and including much of Western Europe. Legions were sent to the outer regions to defend Rome's borders and subdue the warring pagans. They carried advanced skills and culture to the uncivilized Celtic people living in Gaul, Britain and the peninsula of Iberia. The people in the conquered regions were allowed to continue their religious rituals and celebrations, but as new citizens of the Roman Empire they were required to exalt the Emperor and pay an appointed tax.

It was into this pagan world of the Roman Empire that Jesus, the Christian Messiah, was born and later crucified for His teachings and healings. He became the symbol of light, hope, and salvation to many people and replaced the pagan "gods" of the sun, wind, rain, and fire with a monotheistic belief. Christianity was clearly a new religion of infinite spiritual proportion; however, early Christians found it necessary to incorporate elements of heathen practices into their own divine worship and commemorative days in an effort to convert the pagans living within the Empire. In doing so, the pagan and Christian threads of traditions and customs became tightly interwoven.

Early Christians living under Roman jurisdiction refused to worship the Emperor, as dictated by law, and did not participate in public celebrations honoring pagan gods. At first the Romans were tolerant of the Christians' religious beliefs, as long as the allotted tax was paid; but their humble teachings of love, patience and charity were neither understood nor trusted. During the 2nd century, after the death of Christ, turbulent times arose. The four-thousand-year-old Roman Empire was forced to defend its borders against countless barbaric attacks. Although the Church had no part in the border assaults, the superstitious Romans blamed the ill fate of the Empire on the Christians' stubborn refusal to pay tribute to the gods. Consequently, their gatherings were considered acts of conspiracy against the Roman government and the poor Christians suffered several centuries of persecution.

Christianity continued to spread throughout the Roman Empire in spite of the oppression endured by its beleaguered followers until the time of Constantine the Great. His reign marks an important turning point in the development of the Christian Church. Like most Romans, Constantine worshipped the sun in hopes of utilizing its strength. Consistent with legend, Constantine saw a cross imposed on the sun and the words, "In hoc signo vinces" (In this sign shalt thou conquer). He believed this to be a message from the Christian God. With encouragement from his Christian mother (St. Helena), Constantine ordered Christ's emblem C H and R to be displayed on the shields of all his men. And conquer he did. By the early 4th century, Constantine had claimed the emperor's title and had supreme rule over both the East and the West regions of the Roman Empire.

In an effort to better govern and defend his vast domain, Constantine moved the capital to a more suitable location. A "new Rome" was built at the site of ancient Byzantium. The city was renamed Constantinople (present-day Istanbul) in honor of Constantine and dedicated to the Blessed Virgin. This prime location was situated at the crossroads of overland trade routes to the Orient and nearer to the more advanced Greek and Arabic cultures. Although the beautiful new capital was the main residence of Emperor Constantine, after his death, the Empire again divided with capitals established in both Rome and Constantinople.

Even though Constantine did not become a Christian until just before his death in 337, he had decreed toleration of the religion during the early years of his reign. It is believed by some historians that this action was probably motivated by a political interest in the growing numbers of Christians rather than from sympathy for their persecution. Constantine also presided at the opening of the Council of Nicaea in 325. Its purpose was to establish the doctrine of the Christian Church. During the years of persecution, many different beliefs and practices had developed because of the need for secrecy. Therefore, the council of bishops formulated the Nicene Creed, considered by many to be the official profession of Christian faith.

At the close of the 4th century, the Christian Church had became firmly entrenched as the state religion of the Roman Empire with two major divisions, the Western Church centered in Rome and the Eastern Church in Constantinople. There was constant contention, however, between the two concerning who had ultimate authority in Church matters. The Bishop of Rome believed he was in direct succession from St. Peter (considered to be the first Pope), and therefore heir to supreme ecclesiastical power over all Christians. The Patriarch, head of the Church in Constantinople, believed he held supreme rule because he was at the seat of the government. The result was a political and religious power struggle that eventually split the Christian Church into the Roman Catholics and the Eastern Orthodox.

St. Nicholas, the Bishop of Myra

In spite of East-West differences, converting the pagans to Christianity was the most important task of the Church. Because Christ's immediate Second Coming was expected by the early Christians, celebrations of any kind seemed inappropriate. However, as time passed, the Church began to acknowledge dates on which certain martyrs had died. These hallowed days were called Feast Days and quietly acclaimed each Christian martyr's "birthday in heaven." Paying homage in this way was in sharp contrast to the lengthy reveling of the pagans.

One notable Christian martyr from Asia Minor was **Nicholas, the Bishop of Myra,** who died on December 6, 343. Stories circulated about the bishop's generosity and good deeds, and he was credited with performing numerous miracles. Six hundred years after his death, the Bishop was canonized by the Church and he became known as St. Nicholas.

The custom of leaving gifts in stockings which are hung by the fireplace is most often associated with the legend of St. Nicholas and the three maidens. In the town where Nicholas lived, an impoverished merchant had no money for dowries for his daughters and feared having to sell them into slavery, as was the custom of that time. Nicholas took pity on the family. During the cover of night, he rode on a white horse to the poor man's house. He climbed to the rooftop and dropped three bags of gold down the chimney. The anonymous gifts fell into the young maidens' stockings which were left hanging by the hearth to dry. Thus, many children the world over hang stocking in hopes of having them filled with small gifts from the one who comes in secret.

A week before his December 6, Feast Day celebration, the 16th century Dutch Sinterklaas (St. Nicholas) traditionally arrived in Holland from Spain on a ship laden with gifts. With crosier in hand, he mounted a white horse and led a procession through the streets. The saint wore a miter and the red and white ecclesiastical robes of a bishop. With a Moorish helper by his side, Sinterklaas quizzed the children about their behavior and promised to bring them gifts on the eve of St. Nicholas Day.

Lucia, a young woman from Sicily, was accused of conspiracy against the Roman government and condemned to death for her actions. Wearing a crown of candles upon her head to light the dark pathway, Lucia had secretly carried baskets of food to the starving Christians who sought refuge from the Romans in the winding underground catacombs. Stories of Lucia's kindness and bravery circulated throughout the region, and she was credited with enacting miracles. Centuries after her death, Lucia was recognized as a saint by the Church.

The popularity of **St. Lucia** as a Christmas figure is owed to Sweden. According to legend, St. Lucia appeared to starving Swedish peasants during a terrible famine in the Middle Ages. From across a misty lake, Lucia was a vision of hope in glistening white as she ascended from a large ship brimming with food. Around her head was a circle of light.

Lucia's Feast Day is celebrated on December 13, the national holiday in Sweden which officially opens the Christmas season. Old Swedish customs are relived each year in commemoration of their beloved St. Lucy. Before daybreak the eldest daughter in each household dresses in white and places a crown of evergreens and candles on her head. Dutifully, she serves hot coffee and special saffron buns called "lussekatters" to her family.

The bough of greenery on St. Lucia's head contained four candles representing the four Sundays in Advent.

Wanting to draw more people to the Christian religion, Church fathers revised their stance against celebrations by adding to the Church calendar holidays which coincided with seasonal pagan festivities. The nature and dates of these celebrations, instead, only extended the discord within the Church. "The Feast of Epiphany" was selected by the Eastern Church to honor the arrival of the gift-bearing Magi in Bethlehem. This January 6 celebration day superseded the ancient pagan festivals honoring the river and water gods. Meanwhile, the Western Church designated December 25 as "The Feast of the Nativity," or "The Birthday of Our Lord." This Christian holy day aligned with the birthday of the Persian sun god, Mithra; Mithraism was a rival religion especially popular among the Roman soldiers. The Feast Day also fell within the mid-winter festival of Saturnalia and the new year celebration of the Calends.

Over time, Christians in the West recognized January 6 as a holy day and the Eastern Church honored December 25. By 380, the days between the two celebrations were proclaimed a sacred and festive season. The Church intended for the additional celebrations to be reverent occasions but could not completely erase the old pagan customs of their new converts.

In the dark of night, St. Lucia carried baskets of food to Christians hiding in the catacombs.

*M*any pagans who found their way from polytheism to the worship of one God persisted in embracing the spirit of former celebrations, like Saturnalia and the Calends. The merry cheer of Saturnalia was the most jubilant time of the Roman year. This ancient celebration was held in honor of Saturn, the god of Agriculture, and commemorated his reign of peace and prosperity during Italy's mythological Golden Age. The event was marked by the entertaining custom of reversals. Slaves were given brief freedom to drink and gamble, forbidden practices at any other time of the year. They were allowed to dress in their masters' clothing. A servant was chosen to rule the Roman household with nonsensical requests while being waited upon by members of the family.

The pretend reversal of rank and its make-believe anarchy had its origins in customs which existed long before the Romans, Christians, or Church fathers. Many ancient civilizations celebrated the mid-winter season with great exuberance, gory rituals, and complete disregard for order. Kings were looked upon as a link between the human world and the realm of deities, and were sometimes sacrificed to the gods because of their elevated status among mortal men. The kingly sacrifices usually took place when the pagans suffered from natural disasters or when the threat of famine existed. Their sacred ashes were scattered over the fields to ensure fertility for the coming new year.

In time, a "substitute" for the king was chosen from the lower classes. The mock king enjoyed the privileges of being ruler for one week, after which he was sacrificed. These brutal sacrifices finally ceased, but a fictitious role exchange between the master and his slave survived in the celebration of Saturnalia.

Through the centuries the one-day Saturnalian festival developed into a week-long period of celebration from December 17 to 24. The festivities were best known for their extravagant banquets and unrestrained behavior. All businesses closed, except those related to the festivities, just as they do during the Christmas holidays in every corner of the Christian world today. Only the first day had any religious importance. The carousing spirit of the Roman celebration expanded to include all men, free or slave. Evolving from the customs of role reversal between master and slave, a mock **King of Saturnalia** was chosen to lead the frivolity of the games, fairs, and banquets, and his every command had to be obeyed. The festival monarch was draped in a loose fitting, multi-colored tunic instead of the typical white toga worn by the upper classes.

In this topsy-turvy time, men were found parading in the streets dressed in women's clothing or wearing grotesque animal masks and pelts. To the pagans, masquerading was intended to purify family shelters and fields. Loud noises, outlandish costumes, and boisterous shenanigans which accompanied the festivities were thought to confuse and frighten pagan underworld spirits believed to roam about during this uncertain time of year. These frolicsome disguises evolved into the popular mumming traditions during medieval Christmas festivities. Even today, traces of these centuries-old customs can be seen in the Mummer's Parade and Mardi Gras celebrations.

*F*ollowing Saturnalia, the Romans welcomed in the Calends or new year with a celebration from December 31 through January 4. The Calends were associated with the Juvenalia festival of childhood and youth and were characterized by more feasts, processions, songs, candles, decorations, and gifts. It was

The pretentious Roman King of Saturnalia ruled supreme with comical commands.

The candle, wreath, and doll were popular gifts among the Romans during the Calends.

customary for **The Roman** to drape his home and entranceway with garlands of greenery, and gilt fruits and flowers in honor of the gods. Today we enjoy similar decorations during the Christmas holidays. Woodsy scents of pine and balsam waft through the air while garlands of running cedar, holly and other evergreens grace mantles, tables and sideboards.

Gift-giving, the most cherished of our Christmas traditions, has origins in these pre-Christian, new year customs. The Calends were a time of unusual generosity when everyone gave and received mementos representing good luck or wealth in the new year. Teachers received gifts from their students; slaves gave gifts to their masters; even the Emperor expected presents from every citizen. Simple remembrances of laurel branches from the sacred grove of Strenia symbolized continuous life, health, and strength. As the custom of giving evolved, the gifts of laurel were replaced with honey, fruits and cakes, or toys and marbles. Romans of wealth gave gold coins for good luck. In many regions of the world today, people still exchange gifts during New Year celebrations instead of Christmas.

Just as mirth was seen as a means of chasing evil forces back to the underworld, blazing fires shared a kindred role. Extra illumination was deemed a necessity to help ward off spirits lurking in the darkness of the winter solstice. Gifts of candles and oil lamps became popular during Saturnalia and the Calends and were always kept burning to help safeguard the Roman home.

The doll was a special seasonal gift, too, as it always has been. Many a rag doll, wooden doll and china doll have found love cradled in a little girl's arms on Christmas morning. In Roman times clay dolls, called sigillaria, were exchanged during Saturnalia. Children played with the little clay figurines and mothers decorated their homes with them.

Christmas, a time of faith and festivity, took on a different posture as the Church rethought and rearranged its holy days to suit the demands of each century. What remained from these changes were the reveling spirit and cheer displayed during the Roman Saturnalia, plus the customs of decorating and gift giving that stemmed from the generosity expressed during the Calends. Even our tradition of decorating Christmas trees can be traced to the old Roman custom of hanging trinkets and candles on trees believed to be inhabited by pagan spirits. The mid-winter celebrations were the happiest days of the Romans' year, just as Christmastide is the most joyful season of the year for us.

As autumn turns to winter and preparations for the holidays begin, let our thoughts revert to past times. Pause to reflect on those pagan festivals which brightened the long drab days of winter and to the years when early Church fathers struggled to keep Christianity alive. For it was during those "ancient of days" that the fragile new threads of Christianity were knotted to the worn threads of pagan customs and traditions, thus forming the framework of the Christmas tapestry we have inherited.

Light in a Dark Age

Elements of Rome's pagan celebrations — gift giving, candle lighting, and decorating — were woven into the spirit of the Christmas season and into the festive entrance of the new year. Added to this Roman-Christian foundation were strands of superstitious Celtic observances and magical threads from high-spirited Germanic winter fests of Northern Europe.

The Church made every effort to spread the new faith to the heathens of the vast Empire by sending missionaries to the distant regions of Gaul, Iberia, and Britain during the 4th century. In doing so, "The Feast of the Nativity" integrated with various winter festivities of the Celtic people in these remote areas. While Christian missionaries were teaching and preaching to the pagans within the Roman world, there was a restless stirring of Germanic barbarians in the forests outside the Empire.

For centuries minor skirmishes had occurred along the Rhine River, a natural boundary separating the Roman Empire and Celts from the barbarous Germanic tribes of the northlands. As the Roman legions began to weaken from the continual fighting, some of the hardy Germanic attackers were recruited to help safeguard Rome's crumbling borders. Nevertheless, in the early 5th century, hordes of other Germanic tribes broke the defenses and overran their more civilized Roman neighbors while the brutal Huns advanced westward into Eastern Europe from Central Asia.

During these years, the Church struggled alongside the emperors to save the once great Roman capital from invasion as well as from the local peasants themselves. In spite of Church efforts, Rome was sacked several times by the furious onslaughts of Goths, Vandals and Huns who robbed the city of its treasures. Ironically, Odoacer, a German recruit in the Roman legions who rose to the rank of general, deposed the emperor of the West and declared himself master of Italy. With the final fall of Rome and its emperor in 476, Western Europe lapsed into centuries of chaos under the cruel and destructive behavior of barbaric chieftains. Christianity, culture, and art were almost buried under ignorance and superstition.

Never giving up hope, the Roman Church and its missionaries worked diligently to bring the light of Christ to the heathens of Western Europe. As pagan tribes were converted to Christianity and adapted to a more civilized way of life, a unique mixed culture slowly developed. In this long and arduous process of Christian conversion, threads of many delightful pagan customs from the Celtic and Germanic people were woven into an increasingly complex tapestry of Christian traditions. Their old legends tell of mythical gift-bearing gods and goddesses such as Odin, Berchta, and Holda who in many ways parallel our present-day Santa Claus, and for this reason are especially endearing.

Of the many diverse Germanic tribes in Europe, the Franks who settled in Gaul became the most powerful after the fall of the Western Roman Empire. Just as Constantine helped to develop early Christianity in Roman times, Clovis, King of the Franks, was instrumental in spreading the Christian faith among the pagans of Western Europe during the Dark Ages. Legend recounts how Clovis, feeling betrayed by his pagan gods, prayed to his wife's Christian God for victory in battle. The king's prayers were answered for he won many fights thereafter. In keeping with his new-found faith, Clovis was baptized in Reims on Christmas Day in 496, along with three thousand of his people.

Clovis sent missionaries to the surrounding kingdoms to demand acceptance of his new religion. The Emperor of the Eastern Roman Empire, now referred to as the Byzantine Empire, wanted to initiate an alliance with this powerful young leader of the Franks; therefore, he appointed Clovis a Roman consul. This crucial agreement almost certainly helped speed the process of developing order and civility in Europe as the Church continued to expand its influence.

Christianity was established in Ireland during the 5th century by St. Patrick. This small island country was spared the havoc created in Europe by the encroachment of Germanic tribes who never ventured further west than neighboring Britain. The upshot of this isolation was the formation of an Irish Christian Church that continued to grow in strong Celtic traditions during an age of cultural and social darkness, becoming the center of Christian study in Europe after the demise of the Western Roman Empire.

During this "Golden Age" of Ireland, monks recorded numerous sailing adventures of brave saints who were seeking places of seclusion. The tales, or Imramha, are not considered historic, but some truths can be found within the religious embellishments. The most famous of these Irish anchorites was St. Brendan who sailed the unknown Atlantic Ocean sometime between the 5th and 6th centuries. There are those who believe St. Brendan may have been the first white man to reach the New World. Whether true or not, the Imramha were probably the earliest known writings to catch the imagination of Europeans.

The Irish Church was the first to send missionaries to the northern shores of Britain, followed in the 6th century by the Roman Church which sent Augustine and a group of monks to the southern regions. Augustine complied with instructions from the Pope to accept harmless pagan customs when possible and to give Christian interpretation to heathen practices if necessary. With these directives, Augustine set about to convert the Germanic Anglo-Saxons who had overrun the British Isles.

Before Augustine and other missionaries introduced Christianity, the Germanic tribes of Northern Europe celebrated the annual rebirth of the sun with twelve days of festivities. The winter solstice marked the day on which the sun made its turn around from the many long months of darkness. It was a time of joyful celebration called Yuletide and derived its name from "hweolor-tid" which means turning time.

Like all ancient people, the pagans of the North performed ceremonies to ensure the return of light and life during the winter. Because winter days were much shorter and the nights, longer and colder in the North, religious rituals were enacted with more urgency than those performed by their southern counterparts. Fire, sometimes described as "the sun on earth" or "brother to the sun," was a main focus in the solstice celebrations. Ancient revelers, masked or draped in animal skins, performed ritual dances around blazing fires in the huge communal halls.

When assured the sun would survive the winter and new life would be brought to the spring season, the rowdy Yule celebrants rang in the new year with feasting, drinking, and singing. Cattle, which could not be fed through the cold and harsh winter, provided proper sacrifices to the gods, as well as ample meat for the feasts. Abundant ale brewed from the fall harvest flowed freely during the wild Yuletide festivities.

After the pagans were converted to Christianity, mid-winter celebrations were allowed to continue, but sacrifices to the pagan gods were no longer performed. The Christian God was given praise at the Yuletide celebrations for meat provided from the thinning of the herds in preparation for winter. Old pagan shrines decorated with ivy and holly were not destroyed but were turned into places of Christian worship. The Church interpreted the half-man, half-beast pagan gods as devils instead of divinities. Still after fifteen hundred years, the mention of the devil conjures up the same vision created so long ago — that of a frightening dark, horned, animal-like creature.

The Christian holy season of the birth of Christ fell within the twelve days of the Germanic Yule, and the festivities of the two celebrations gradually meshed. New Christian converts celebrated Christ's mass in the same exuberant manner that they had celebrated the rebirth of the sun. Holy days were filled with customs of heathen worship and ancient superstitions which no longer held their original significance.

In some regions, great community bonfires were kept ablaze for twelve days during the "Yuletide season." In other areas, Yule logs were dragged into each home on Christmas Eve. A log, large enough to burn continuously for twelve days, was superstitiously lit from the previous year's shard. For some, the magical powers of the burning log destroyed all hatreds and misunderstandings. Its ashes were scattered over the fields to help guarantee a good harvest for the subsequent season. Although we no longer burn a twelve-day yule log, we do enjoy the warmth of a good fire during the holidays. For some mysterious reason its glow kindles friendships, family ties, and the spirit of the Christmas season.

Just as the Bible is considered the inspired Word of God, myths were the sacred stories of the pagan Germanic tribes. These myths explained the mysteries of nature long before the introduction of Christianity. Myths or folklore were memorized and handed down by word of mouth from one generation to the next. Adventurous escapades of the gods were described in some stories while others revealed the more serious origins and meanings of death, fire, nature, or creation. Myths were recited during seasonal celebrations and were enhanced with rituals. Many of today's Christmas customs such as caroling, hanging mistletoe, and rewarding children's good behavior with gifts are rooted in old Germanic myths.

Without the benefit of modern science, many imaginative myths gave an explanation of the dreaded winter solstice to the pagans. In some regions of Northern Europe, legend proclaimed that the sun was born each morning, traveled across the sky during the day, and sank into the underworld every night. As the fall season turned to winter and the day's light began to shorten, the ancient people feared the sun was being held captive by the evil spirits of the underworld and all living things would die. To appease the gods and coax the sun's return to the sky, it was customary to sing cheerful songs and give special gifts.

Keeping the homefires burning was an important part of every ancient household. Fire not only provided warmth in the bitter cold Northern winters, but its blaze was thought to dispel evil spirits as well. A thorough cleaning would also rid the house of unwanted goblins and trolls that could come inside during the darkest time of the year. The presence of a hearth goddess in Germanic folklore assured an orderly house.

In some regions it is said that the spirit of Berchta, the goddess of the hearth and domestic chores, descended through the smoke of the fire which burned on an altar made of flat stones. Her presence helped guide the fortune-tellers in seeing the future of those gathered for the feast.

During Yule each dwelling was scrubbed and then decorated with evergreens and fir to honor and welcome the yearly visit of **Berchta,** the fastidious old hearth goddess. Accompanied by her troupe of dark and scary little helpers, Berchta roamed the countryside on a pale horse, checking each cottage for its cleanliness and proper spinning. She rewarded diligent children with a blessing, but curses were placed upon those who neglected their daily chores.

Berchta had a dreadful appearance. With her long crooked nose, large teeth, matted hair, and gigantic feet, she resembled a witch more than a goddess and ruled over night-hags and enchantresses. Although Berchta herself was disheveled, she expected cleanliness and industriousness from everyone else. Despite her haggard image, children who worked hard and obeyed their parents had no reason to fear Berchta.

The legends and superstitious customs of Berchta were eventually woven into the Christian celebration of the birth of Christ. Today, Berchta's feast day is still celebrated on Twelfth Night in parts of Austria, southern Germany and Switzerland. A special supper of pancakes or herring and dumplings is served. If the scraps from the meal are not left on the table for Berchta, the family may suffer terrible consequences.

In many localities berchten are selected to dance and jump about. Sometimes the dancers are divided into two groups, the ugly berchten and beautiful berchten. Dressed in elaborate costumes, they travel from farm to farm and dance about in the fields to symbolically stamp out the evil spirits and to insure future fertility to the land. When the ritual is completed, the berchten are served refreshments. In some regions this ceremony is performed on Shrove Tuesday.

Berchta, the witch-like Germanic goddess, rewarded good little children with a blessing.

As the gracious and tenderhearted goddess, Holda lives on in many German legends and fairytales. Even today when it snows in the Alps, there are some who say Holda or Frau Holle is making her down bed because the feathers are flying.

erman gods and goddesses had many names and descriptions depending on the region. Consequently, Berchta was sometimes known as Berkta, Bertha, Precht, Percht, Perchta, or Hertha (from which comes the term "hearth stones"). The beautiful young sky goddess, Holde, was Berchta's counterpart in Northern Germany and their legends have been combined over the centuries with many other folkloric figures to create characters ranging from the benevolent White Lady to a wicked witch. Even though they appeared to be quite opposite, Holda and Berchta shared a common bond — household order and spinning.

Holde was also known as Holle, Hulle, Hulda, Holl, or Holda. Manifested as **Holda,** the goddess was a kind and helpful being. She came to earth during the Yule celebrations dressed in a glistening white cape of goose feathers. She could be seen herding her flock of geese through the narrow streets. Feathers that fell from her cape were magically transformed into gold coins, which Holda kindly gave to the hard-working mountain villagers. As the gracious and tenderhearted goddess, Holda lives on in many German legends and fairytales.

Legends of the hearth goddess were spread throughout Europe by the invading Germanic tribes during the Dark Ages. With the coming of Christianity, Berchta's stories were blended with religious celebrations. Her impact was evident in subsequent characters such as Italy's Befana and Russia's Baboushka. Berchta's scraggly group of followers became helpers to St. Nicholas in some regions of Europe. Stories of the old hearth goddess were clouded by both Christian and Moorish influences on the Iberian peninsula. Berchta faded to obscurity in Spanish lore, but her dark and mysterious companions lived on to become entangled with the saga of the Three Kings.

Holda, the German goddess of the sky, descended to earth during Yule celebrations dressed in a beautiful, white feather cape.

*In Scandinavia the ancient barn elves or nisser were the protectors of the farm animals. But for all their help, the household had to deal with annoying pranks performed by these invisible little creatures who lived in the attics or under the floorboards. After the Reformation the invisible dancing dwarfs became the gift givers during the Christmas season. The Danish gnome of Christmas, **Julenisse,** wore a red stocking cap and had a long white beard. The children ceremoniously put out a bowl of hot porridge or rice pudding called "Julgrot" for Julenisse on Christmas Eve. Any break in this tradition was thought to bring bad luck and a poor harvest for the coming season. In turn the nisse hid presents around the house. Santa's elfish helpers of today can trace their origins to these invisible mischief makers of ancient days.*

In addition to the melding of characters and their singular traits, customs ranging from the art of baking to the symbolic colors displayed during the holidays crossed borders and cultures and eventually settled into our own celebrations. Today's Christmas season just isn't complete without the aroma of fresh baked cookies cut into ornamental shapes and decorated with sprinkles or icing. Even this simple tradition, handed down to us by our parents and grandparents, has a thread of familiarity with the mid-winter customs of pagan Europe. In ancient times special cakes and breads were baked in an effort to gain favor with the field gods.

Mistletoe, another popular feature of our Christmas celebrations, played an important role in ancient pagan ceremonies. This rootless plant which thrives in the barren trees of winter was revered by both the Celtic and Germanic tribes. It was symbolic of the unexplained link between the heavenly power of the sun and the earth's vegetation. Because of its magical powers, mistletoe was the focus of special rituals performed during mid-winter celebrations. Druid priests clipped the sacred greenery from the oak trees, never letting its leaves touch the ground. It was then cut into many small pieces and shared among the people. Each sprig of mistletoe brought good fortune and blessings to the recipient and was hung in every household to protect it against evil spirits during the winter solstice.

Another especially important quality of the mistletoe, which has been woven into our Christmas tapestry, is that of peace and good will. According to Norse legend, a sprig of mistletoe inflicted a deadly wound on Balder, the sun god. This event occurred during the mythological "Peacestead," a season of tranquility and humanity, which prevented the punishment of the sun god's brother, the blind god of darkness who had been tricked into committing this shameful act by the jealous god of fire. The deadly mistletoe thus became a symbol of peace. Gifts were placed on Balder's bier, and in turn, the sun god sent presents to his mourners from the realm of darkness.

Through the years mistletoe continued to symbolize peace. Enemies congregated beneath the hanging green ball dotted with white berries to settle their disputes. Some believe making up differences under the magical powers of the mistletoe inspired our romantic Christmas custom of stealing a kiss underneath it. Whatever the reason, hanging mistletoe in our homes during Christmas is, without a doubt, a remnant of pagan traditions.

The predominant red and green colors found in so many Christmas decorations also have pagan origins. Evergreens were symbolic of continued life and the growth of crops, and the red blood of livestock represented fertility. Fertility rites were a very important part of heathen worship as man's survival depended upon the reproduction of both plants and animals. With Christian interpretation, the dark green holly leaf became symbolic of the everlasting life of Christ, and its cluster of red berries represented His blood shed for our sins; however, the Church declared white to be the true color of Christmas because it stood for purity.

Although fervent missionaries were busy instructing pagans in Christian principals, they were not alone in their efforts to convert the world to monotheism. The strict teachings of Muhammad, founder of Islam in the 7th century, conflicted with Christian doctrine and posed a constant threat to Europe and Christianity. Within a century the teachings of Mohammed had spread across Northern Africa. In quest of Western Europe, the Moslem Arabs crossed the Strait of Gibraltar and overran the Gothic Kingdom in Spain, thus bringing the Islamic faith into a predominately Roman Catholic realm.

After a major defeat of the scimitar-wielding Arabs by the axe-battling Franks in 732, Charles Martel was touted the savior of Western Christendom. The Frankish king pushed the Moors back into Spain where they remained for eight hundred years. With victory over the Moors came prestige and power for Charles Martel, who used his new authority to confiscate Church properties. He divided these lands among the nobility; in return, the nobles pledged allegiance to their Christian king. These oaths marked the beginning of the feudal system and the Christian way of life which prevailed in Europe throughout the Middle Ages.

Within one hundred years a mighty Frankish Empire from the Mediterranean to Scandinavia was ruled by Charlemagne, known as Charles the Great. Hoping to secure protection from the ever-present Moslem threat, the Pope crowned Charlemagne "Holy Roman Emperor,"

the first in over four hundred years. During his fifty-year reign, Western Europe prospered, and it appeared that the old Roman Empire had been resurrected; but peace was short lived as the vast Frankish Empire was divided into smaller king-doms following Charlemagne's death. In 962, King Otto, a strong defender of the Pope, was crowned Emperor of the West, which officially marked the birth of the "Holy Roman Empire of the German Nation." This Empire, as all others before it, was not so very holy, and unfortunately, fighting continued to plague Western Europe.

Christianity was well established in Western Europe by the 9th century. Pagan believers in the spirit world and fertility rites had been converted, and the Church assumed total responsibility for Christian life. The recovery from hundreds of years of turmoil to a peaceful existence was abruptly halted by fierce Scandinavian sea rovers from the North. For two more centuries the people of the coastal villages of Western Europe suffered at the hands of the Vikings. Churches and monasteries were favorite targets of these marauders because of the elaborate gold and silver objects stored there. The stolen bounty was then used to purchase the lands they ransacked. In the course of time, the Vikings settled into Celtic-Roman Christian society and added yet another influence to the cultures of France, England, and Ireland.

Odin, the Vikings' All-Father god, rewarded his people with gifts of fruits and nuts during Yule celebrations.

ustoms and traditions surrounding **Odin**, the Vikings' All-Father god, were incorporated into the Christian celebration of the birth of Jesus. According to the *Eddas,* Norse mythology recorded in Iceland during the Middle Ages, Odin was a descendant of the ancient king of gods in Asia who wandered across the cold and barren regions of Northern Europe. This creator of the world and mankind, this inventor of runes, wisdom, magic, poetry, prophecy, sun, rain, and culture, reigned over all the other gods. Odin left sons to rule in each land visited, from Russia and Saxland to Frankland, Jutland, Sweden, and Norway. He was known by as many as two hundred names, depending on the region, and many noble families claimed to be his descendants. To the Anglo-Saxons, he was know as Woden and the Germans called him Wodan. But to the Scandinavians he was Odin. He wore an eye patch because he gave one eye in search of wisdom. Two ravens perched upon his shoulder kept him informed of earthly events.

During the endlessly bleak and dreary Scandinavian winters, when weather prevented the seafarers from going "a-viking," everyone participated in a great Yule celebration. Sacrifices were made to their All-Father god to hasten the sun's return. Covered in a mantle of fur, the white-bearded Odin descended to earth during the twelve days of festivities on a beautiful white horse. He rode through the dark and icy northlands, rewarding his people with gifts of fruits, nuts, good fortune, and health. Children placed their shoes, brimming with carrots and hay, beside the door for Odin's horse. To the children's delight, small gifts were found in their shoes the following morning. Bits of Odin's legend were mixed with legends of St. Nicholas in later centuries.

name Russia. Exploring the inland rivers, the Russians set up a prosperous trade with the Byzantines, who had a major influence in the development of Russian culture and its Eastern Orthodox religion.

Early Russian chronicles tell how Vladimir, a pagan, sent envoys to research the different religions of the world. They were unimpressed with Western Christianity, believed Judaism would be unsuitable, and rejected Islam because of its prohibition of alcohol; however, their reports of the splendor of the Greek Orthodox basilica, Hagia Sophia, convinced Vladimir that this was the religion for his people. Vladimir and the whole city of Kiev were baptized along the banks of the Dnieper River in 988.

A beautiful icon of St. Nicholas was brought to Kiev from Constantinople, along with marvelous legends surrounding the life of the saint and his miracles. The stories were adapted to the colorful Russian culture. St. Nicholas became the beloved protector of the weak and poor Russian peasants, and his Feast Day was celebrated on December 6 with ardent devotion for centuries.

Christmas and the customs of the legendary **Kolya** (the Russian version of St. Nicholas) have not been recognized openly since the time of the powerful czars. Russia's Revolution at the turn of the 19th century altered Christmas celebrations in this part of the world. Children growing up in Russia did not celebrate the religious Christmas holidays but enjoyed remnants of old customs that peered through newer adaptations. A visit from Grandfather Frost on New Year's Eve replaced St. Nicholas, and a New Year tree was trimmed instead of the Christmas tree. The most recent political developments have opened the doors of many old Russian churches and, hopefully, a treasure-trove of Christmas traditions for future generations as well.

Kolya of Russia

During the time Western Europe was coping with the coastal Viking raids, another group of Scandinavian seafarers set sail eastward to northernmost Europe and established the colonies of Novgorod and Kiev. These Vikings were known as the Rus, from which comes the

While Russians were being converted to the Eastern Orthodox religion through the influence of the Byzantine Church, the people of Bohemia (present day Czech Republic) were being taught the doctrines of the Catholic Church. The Bohemian prince, Wenceslas, was converted to Roman Christianity at a young age and was known for his kindness and concern for the poor throughout the Kingdom. He founded many churches during his short reign of only four years, but **Good King Wenceslas** also made many enemies among the nobles who were jealous of his devotion and generosity to the Church. The pious king was killed in an assassination plotted by his own mother and brother. Wenceslas became patron saint and protector of the castle and all of Bohemia because of his benevolence and Christian ideals; and to this day, the Czech people hold a festival in his honor on the anniversary of his death. To the rest of the world, though, Wenceslas is best known through the popular Christmas carol, "Good King Wenceslas," written in 1853.

Good King Wenceslas

There was continual controversy over Church doctrine even though the Holy Roman and Byzantine empires, as well as the smaller kingdoms of Europe, shared the same Christian faith. However, doctrine was not the sole reason for the final schism of the Christian church. Political problems compounded by cultural differences between the East and the West were the major underlying causes. A meeting between the Byzantine Patriarch and the Roman Cardinal sent to Constantinople by the Pope in 1053 ended in mutual excommunication and marked the final split of the Christian Church into Eastern Orthodox and Roman Catholic.

By the 11th century Christianity prevailed, without question, as the dominant faith throughout Europe. After the fall of the Roman Empire, the Church had not only managed to survive the upheavals caused by the many invading tribes but tempered the barbarism of those mighty warriors who ruled during the Dark Ages. The clergy, among the few who could read or write during this troubling time, worked laboriously to teach as well as transcribe past culture. Converting pagans to Christianity was a long and difficult struggle but in the process, a larger, more dynamic Christmas tapestry was created, when the magical threads of myth and lore were brought into the Christian celebrations.

Kolya's legend is retold in an old Russian Christmas carol. On Holy Night, Kolya trudged through the deep snow from house to house, placing little wheat cakes on the window sill for each member of the household. To ensure good luck for the coming year, these cakes had to be eaten on Christmas morning.

King Wenceslas of Bohemia took pity on a poor peasant man he saw gathering wood in the snow outside the castle walls. On the eve of the Feast of St. Stephen, the good king and his faithful page set out in the cold night air to carry a parcel of meat, wine, and pinelogs to the peasant's unfortunate family. The snow was so deep the young helper had to step in the king's footprints.

The Crusading Spirit

The enthusiastic spirit of Roman Christendom was reflected in the celebrations of the Christmas season during the Middle Ages. Villages and towns all over Europe took part in the glorious festivities which offered an escape from the hard struggles of day to day living. Many lasting characteristics of the holiday were established at that time. It was not until the 11th century, however, that December 25 was called "Christmas," a term derived from the Church's special celebration of the liturgy for this day, Christ's Mass. December 25 to January 6 became popularly known as the "twelve days of Christmas." The four-week period approaching Christmas, called Advent, filled more of winter's dreary days with anticipation of the miraculous event. The tapestry of Christmas traditions expanded even more as Christian pilgrims, journeying about from place to place, absorbed new and wondrous customs.

Every phase of European life was directed by the Church during the Middle Ages. Pilgrimages to shrines or sites significant to the Christian faith were common, and overland journeys to the Holy Land were a particular favorite. Each Christian who entered Jerusalem was charged a fee by the Arab Moslems who controlled the region. These financial arrangements were agreeable to both and worked well until the Turks took over the region. Although they soon became followers of Mohammed, the Seljuk Turks were not as civilized as the Arab Moslems and attacked pilgrim caravans en route to the Holy Land. As the Turks advanced closer and posed a threat to the Eastern Empire, the Byzantines petitioned the Pope in Rome for help.

In response to the plea, and in retaliation for the pilgrims' fate, the Pope encouraged all faithful Christians, including monarchs, knights, common folk, and even children, to unite in a campaign to reclaim the Holy Lands from the Moslem infidels. The Pope's call to arms in 1095 launched a series of Holy Wars called the Crusades. Motives for the crusading redeemers varied from the remission of sin to wealth, power, title, or fame.

It was not long before Western crusaders became hostile to the Byzantine Christians and overtook parts of the Eastern Empire. Animosity between the Eastern and Western Christians had been brewing for centuries as social differences mounted. The Eastern Byzantines had always felt superior to their half-barbaric Roman brothers and thought themselves to be the true Church. On the other hand, Roman Christians in the West considered themselves to be soldiers of the cross and regarded the wealthy Byzantines as weak. Since a crusade was considered to be any mission intended to defend the Pope, it was no surprise when soldiers of the Fourth Crusade sailed from Venice to Constantinople in 1204. The Western Christians sacked and looted the beautiful treasure-filled city and established a "Latin Empire" that lasted for more than fifty years before the Byzantine Empire was reestablished.

The widespread tradition of gift giving is owed in part to the political upheavals during the Crusades. Fearing the Moslem infidels' thieving practices, Italian sailors took the remains of St. Nicholas, Bishop of Myra, from Asia Minor to Bari, Italy, in 1087. St. Nicholas's legends spread from the port town of Bari to other seaports and soon all of Europe knew of his good deeds and generous nature. Numerous churches were built in his honor, and pilgrimages to Bari were not uncommon. Even the familiar surnames of Nichols, Nicholson, Collins, Colson, Niesen, and Nielsen can be traced to the saint's popularity.

Giving gifts on December 6, St. Nicholas Day, originated in France and became an official holiday in Western Europe during the 12th century. Supposedly, nuns in a French convent secretly left bundles filled with fruits, nuts, and oranges at the houses of poor families with small children. Since St. Nicholas's good deeds were so well known, he was assumed to be the anonymous gift bearer. This custom spread quickly to other regions and was enjoyed by both rich and poor.

An essential thread of the gift-giving tradition, derived from Germanic folklore and woven into our tapestry during the Middle Ages, was that of a medieval gift bearer. Wodan, the Germanic All-Father god, disguised himself as an earth-bound wanderer and traveled from village to village with gifts for the excited children during winter solstice celebrations in pagan days. Unlike Odin's Viking attire, Wodan wore a heavy cloak and a broad-brimmed hat and carried a staff as he roamed about on foot. During the lengthy transition from pagan to Christian characters, legends of Wodan and his travels mixed with those of St. Nicholas. The result was a medieval figure with the look of a wanderer but bearing the name of the Saint.

Whether in bishop's accoutrements or wanderer's cloak and staff, the **Medieval St. Nicholas** was depicted with a dark beard in most religious art until the 1300's. While Christian and pagan legends were passed down from one generation to the next in many different languages, parts of one story became disordered and fused with segments of others. Consequently, through many translations, St. Nicholas acquired Odin's snow-white beard, which is still an identifying characteristic of Santa Claus today.

St. Nicholas gradually became the Christian gift bearer throughout Western Europe. Although St. Nicholas came in secret at first, as time went on, he began to make visits openly. His legends not only replaced Odin's, but he also assumed Berchta's role as the admonisher or rewarder of children's behavior. However, the old pagan stories and figures were not entirely erased. As the legend of St. Nicholas evolved during the Middle Ages, the chastising duties acquired from Berchta were delegated to a sinister-looking helper who usually carried a bundle of switches or rods for the saint. Over the centuries these figures took various forms and names such as Black Peter, Knecht Ruprecht, Hansrupart, Rumpaus, Hanscrouf, Jan, Hans Trapp, Cert, Bartel, and Krampas.

The dark-bearded Medieval St. Nicholas looked like a wanderer as he delivered his gifts.

Little ones could sometimes hear the thumping of Befana's heavy sack of toys as she delivered her gifts, even though her magical powers rendered her invisible.

In the 12th century three bodies, thought to be those of the Magi, were discovered in the basilica in Milan. Emperor Barbarossa transferred the bodies to Cologne, where they were enclosed in a beautiful shrine. This discovery rekindled an interest in the Biblical gift-bearing Magi. In Spain the identity of the black king from Ethiopia was confused with St. Nicholas's dark helper. Small children believed Balthazar brought their gifts on Epiphany Eve and smudged their faces with charcoal to indicate that he was there. Eventually, all three kings assumed the gift-giving duties. Even today Spanish children write letters to the Three Kings just as American boys and girls send messages to Santa.

Additional legends of the Magi, which surfaced throughout the Christian world, probably inspired the bewitching stories of Befana and Baboushka. The Italian **Befana** traces her roots to the old Germanic hearth goddess Berchta, whose legends came to Italy during the Dark Ages of barbaric migration. As these people were converted to Christianity, Berchta's character changed to a more suitable Christian one. She was known as Befana, the kind-hearted Christmas witch who appeared every Epiphany Eve to bring gifts to nice children and lumps of coal to naughty ones. Her name is derived from the word Epifania (Italian for Epiphany). Befana Day is celebrated in Italy on January 6.

Christian children everywhere love Befana's legend. The haggard old woman lived in a small cottage in the Tuscan hills of Italy many centuries ago. She had great magical powers and told fortunes. One cold winter day Befana was asked directions to Bethlehem by three Wise Men who were traveling through her village. They invited her to join them in search of a newborn King. The old woman wanted to go but declined their invitation because she had many household chores to do. Not long after the Wise Men had left, Befana changed her mind. Quickly, she snatched her long black cape and boots and went out into the chilly night to catch up with the caravan. On the doorstep she found a large sack filled with toys. Toting this heavy bag on her back, Befana roamed about looking for the Wise Men and the Christ Child but never found them.

After searching for many years, an inner voice told Befana the Baby Jesus was no longer in the manger in Bethlehem, but His spirit could be found within every child. From that time on Befana traveled the countryside on Epiphany Eve leaving small gifts for good little children along the way. Her large bag was always full, but she never tired from the load. Little ones tried to stay awake to see her, but Befana's magical powers made her invisible. Sometimes a bell could be heard, warning the children to hurry to sleep before Befana's arrival.

Befana, Italy's kind-hearted Christmas witch, traveled the countryside on the eve of Epiphany.

The Russian legend of **Baboushka** is similar to that of Befana. As Baboushka swept the snow from her porch, she saw three splendidly dressed foreign kings who were following a bright star pointing the way to Bethlehem and the Christ Child. Baboushka welcomed the royal travelers into her cottage and served them black bread and tea. Baboushka was invited to accompany the Kings on their journey, but she was reluctant to accept the kind invitation because she had many household chores to do.

The following morning a cinnamon scent still lingered in the air reminding Baboushka of her visitors. Feeling guilty about her decision not to go with the Three Kings, Baboushka changed her mind. She hurriedly gathered a few small toys for the Infant and put a piece of black bread in her pocket. Wrapping warmly in her cape and scarf (babushka), Baboushka set out on the long trek through the cold Russian snow in hopes of catching up with the procession. She finally reached Bethlehem, but the manger was empty. Sadly she placed the black bread in the little bed of straw so that He would know that she had come.

Even though Baboushka grew old, she continued her search for the Child King. Every Christmas Baboushka slipped into the bedrooms of sleeping children and left little wooden toys or candy sealed in shiny paper on their pillows. A tear dropped from Baboushka's weary eyes as she peeped into every cradle. There was always a faint scent of cinnamon left in the air after Baboushka's visit.

Although the Holy season was meant to be reverent during the Middle Ages, the holidays were observed with a reveling spirit due to the lingering influences from both the Roman and Germanic peoples. Some pagan customs, which had been given Christian interpretation, became an accepted and even cherished part of the Christmas celebrations. Candles, once used to chase away evil spirits, symbolized Christ, the Light of the World, and illuminated every window as a sign of welcome to Christian travelers. Many other traditions, however, revealed the people's carousing nature. Feasting, singing, and dancing were carried to extremes, and the holiday's religious purpose was virtually lost in all the merriment.

Kings required Christmas gifts from their subjects, the value of which was in accordance with a person's rank. Extravagant presents were exchanged between rulers of countries and among the wealthy who could afford the custom. The poor participated in the less costly festivities of the holiday season such as mumming, which was as popular in the Middle Ages as it had been in the Roman Empire during the celebration of Saturnalia.

Miming, playing a part without words, and guising, wearing a mask, went hand in hand with mumming traditions. The mummers dressed in fringed costumes or wore their clothing inside out. Masks or blackened faces added to their disguise. Recognition of a mummer would break "the luck" performers brought. Groups of masqueraders had free reign as they roved about the villages demanding gifts for their entertainment.

Baboushka kept sweets and small toys in her apron pockets in anticipation of the Christ Child.

The Morris Dance was brought to England from Spain by John of Gaunt. This Moorish dance became an important part of the English "mumming" customs associated with Christmas celebrations during the reign of the House of Tudor (1485-1603). Decorated in streamers of brightly colored ribbons and bells, The Morris Dancer entertained with all sorts of amusements. He was easily identified by the leather band of bells he wore around the calf of his leg. The Morris Dance in Christmas festivities parallels the Fool's Dance at the Roman Saturnalia celebrations. Although it was prohibited by the Puritans along with other holiday festivities in the 17th century, the Morris Dance eventually regained its popularity as an English folk dance.

Legend has it that on the night Christ was born, the animals in the stable at Bethlehem were turned out to make room for Mary, Joseph, and the Baby. The displaced horse roamed about from place to place seeking shelter. In South Wales the wandering horse was known as The **Mari Lwyd**. Every Christmas it was customary for the prancing, dancing Mari Lwyd to lead a procession through the crowded streets. As recognition was sure to bring bad luck, a blanket decorated with bells, baubles, and colorful streamers disguised the bearer of the Mari Lwyd's wooden head which was mounted to a long pole. Her eyes were made of glass and her jaw was constructed with wire to open and snap shut. Strange noises from the "Gray Mare" scared but delighted the little children. Tossing coins into her mouth without being bitten was a sign of good luck, but those who were nipped were given fines. The rowdy group traveled from house to house singing verses of lengthy songs to which an answer was required. After the Mari Lwyd was properly tipped, the troupe was served a Christmas punch.

The Christmas season in medieval Europe was celebrated in some fashion from All Hallow's Eve, October 31, to Candlemas, February 2, with special emphasis on the days between Christmas and Twelfth Night. Medieval courts spent enormous sums to finance gala affairs during the Christmas season. Games such as Dice, Cards, Bowls, and Snap-Dragon, forbidden except at Christmas time, were played between the huge meals. There were pantomimes, processions, tournaments, and songfests that went along with the feasting.

The mumming customs of the poor filtered into the King's court and great manor houses where a **Lord of Misrule** was appointed to direct the holiday festivities. He arranged for elaborate pageants and a variety of entertainment. Depending on the region, the Lord of Misrule was called the King of Christmas, the King of Bean, the Abbot of Unreason, the Christmas Prince, or the l'Abbe de la Malgouverne. Whatever his title, he was always the monarch of revels during holiday celebrations. This character, originating from the ancient pagan customs of role reversal, was the counterpart of the Roman King of Saturnalia. And just like the old Roman, the Lord of Misrule's every command, no matter how ludicrous, had to be obeyed.

Much of nature was still a mystery during the Middle Ages, and many superstitious customs rooted in pagan ignorance were allowed by the Church if they did not contradict Christian doctrine. Of particular interest were the unusual happenings that supposedly took place the night of the miracle birth. It was believed that ghosts, witches, and other evil spirits were rendered powerless on Christmas Eve. Stories circulated about animals speaking at midnight and flowers blooming in the dead of winter, yet no one could prove these events.

One quaint Christian story relates the miracle of the Christmas rose. A poor peasant family had been cast out of their village and was living in the distant Forest of Goinge. As the Christmas season neared, the parents were saddened for they had no gifts to give their children. But a wonderful miracle took place on that cold Christmas Eve. Upon waking the next morning, the children were delighted to find an enchanted forest of colorful roses which bloomed that one special day.

The eve of the Twelfth Day of Christmas was a time for more resolute customs which centered around the traditional English cider ale. To ensure the health of growing things which laid dormant in winter, farmers gathered in the orchards to sprinkle wassail on the roots of the apple trees and place bread in the branches. Their boisterous songs were intended to wake up the spirits thought to live in the trees. The word 'wassail' originates from the Anglo-Saxon *wes hal* which meant 'be whole' and was used as a toast to one another's health. Every English family had a simmering bowl of wassail on the fire during the Christmas season. In some regions it was tradition to "go wassailing" from house to house carrying a bowl decorated with ribbons and garlands. After drinking toasts to the season, the bowl was refilled. This custom tended to increase the "cheerfulness" of the season.

The revelous spirit of the old medieval Christmas festivities are found in several of today's seasonal celebrations. On New Year's Eve in Times Square, masses of people jam the streets to dance to loud, festive music. When the ball drops, officially signaling the start of a new year, the crowd roars and the band strikes up the

Guests at the royal courts were entertained by minstrels, costumed maskers, or by the antics of the Lord of Misrule himself. Dressed in gaudy, parti-colored costume, he paraded about carrying a ribbon-trimmed scepter and amused his audience with riddles, pranks, and pantomimes. A pointed velvet cap, decorated with a feather and sprig of greenery, covered his head; a stiff lace ruff encircled his neck; a short satin cape draped about his shoulders. Those who dared to disobey the bizarre demands from the Lord of Misrule received absurd punishments for the amusement of other guests.

tune of 'Auld Lange Syne.' Mumming moved from the Christmas season to became a part of the pre-Lenten Carnival in Southern Europe known to us as Mardi Gras. The mid-winter festival of Samhain in England and the German custom of Belsnickeling survived in our Halloween. These old traditions are played out by children dressed in costumes who go door to door seeking sweets, leery of ghostly shadows and ghoulish sounds in the night, and just as fearful as our ancient ancestors. The spirited pranks of our children, which follow the cries of "trick or treat" on October 31, mark the beginning of our modern-day season of festivity that lingers through January.

The Church taught Christian doctrine by staging miracle plays which were performed in Latin by the clergy. The Paradise Play, representing the creation of man and his expulsion from Paradise, was a favorite production during Advent. In time the Church could no longer accommodate the large crowds attracted by the play's popularity. Once removed from the Church and its control, the performances grew into worldly extravaganzas. Paid actors replaced the clergy, and the beautiful religious dramas deteriorated into mockeries.

The religious aspects of the Holy season were most certainly overshadowed by superstition and wild revelry displayed during celebrations in the Middle Ages. Attempting to make Christmas a more reverent occasion, **St. Francis of Assisi** staged the first living Nativity where a special mass was held in 1223. A more spiritual emphasis returned to the Christmas celebration as the popularity of this production spread through Europe. The events which took place in Bethlehem so long ago still hold appeal for people all over the world. Pageants are presented in churches,

and Nativity scenes made of wood, porcelain, clay, or paper mache are found beneath many a Christmas tree during this holiest of seasons.

St. Francis revived the religious devotion and charity shown by the early Christians, while preserving an earnest respect for the Church and its hierarchy. This rejuvenated spirit among the people may have helped to extend the supremacy of the Catholic Church in Western Europe a while longer by calming the rumbling voices of dissatisfaction which were beginning to surface. Some historians believe the reform movements of the 16th century would have occurred several centuries earlier had it not been for St. Francis.

While the people of Western Europe were preoccupied with the Crusades, armies of brutal Mongols from the Asian plains were occupied with building a mega-empire which stretched from China to Russia. Oddly enough, the great Mongolian leader, Kublai Khan, was interested in European customs and religious beliefs and encouraged contacts with Western travelers and merchants. In 1273, through the aid of Venetian traders, Kublai Khan sent a message to the Pope requesting at least one hundred Christian scholars to be sent to the Mongolian capital to explain the doctrines of Christianity. These religious teachers were to accompany the Venetians on their return trip.

The merchants did indeed return to the palace of the Khan two years later, but no scholars were among them. Only two papal emissaries were sent in response to the Kahn's petition and part way into the long and dangerous journey, even they turned back in fear. However, the expedition had some merit because Marco Polo, who had accompanied his father on the return voyage, found favor with the Great Khan. The

St. Francis made a lasting impression on the illiterate population of Greccio, Italy, and elsewhere by using the villagers and live animals to recreate the miracle birth. Many churches, inspired by the saint's resourcefulness, presented the Nativity year after year. As time passed, craftsmen hand-carved miniatures of the Nativity which decorated many homes, and artists were commissioned to construct elaborate manger scenes for the royal courts. Each year the displays grew larger as figures portraying the different social classes were added.

For many centuries, the Mongolian tribes recognized the year's end with a celebration called Herdsmen's Day. Even on the remote Asian plains, it was customary to exchange small trinkets or gifts during the festivities. The Chinese god, Tasi Sen Yeh, carried a sack of toys on his back and gave gifts of money to the children at the year's end. Today only about one percent of the Chinese population is Christian. But even as far away as China, the celebration of Christmas is enhanced by an Asian Gift Bearer. Lan Khoong-Khoong, a Christian character whose name means "Nice Old Father," leaves gifts in muslin stockings for the celebration of Sheng Dan Jieh or "Holy Birth Festival."

young Venetian was sent on many diplomatic missions throughout the immense Mongol Empire over a twenty-year span.

Western culture and religious beliefs, which had so intrigued the Khan, actually had very little influence on his empire. But through Marco Polo's recorded experiences of the most extraordinary travels in all of history, Europeans learned of customs of an ancient Chinese people and cultivated an interest in adventure. Within a few centuries, numerous voyages to unknown continents carried Western culture and Christianity to the far corners of the world.

Slowly, the Catholics in Spain won back the territories taken by the Arabs in the 8th century. With each small victory a Christian kingdom was established until all of Spain was under one ruler and, more importantly, under one Church. Determined that Christianity should prevail, all Moslems and Jews were required to accept the faith of the Catholic Church or be exiled.

While the Roman Catholics of Spain were successfully reclaiming their lands from the Arab Moslems, the one-thousand-year-old Byzantine Empire was gradually being chiseled away by the Moslem Turks. Finally, in 1453, Constantinople became the new capital of the Turkish Ottoman Empire. Unlike the Moslem and Jewish people in Spain, Christians in the Turkish Empire were allowed to stay and continue their traditional form of worship; even so, they suffered the consequences of unusual Moslem laws and customs. For example, every four years young Christian children were "lawfully" taken from their homes and forced into servitude.

One legend of St. Nicholas in particular reflects the injustices of the Moslem laws. A young Christian boy named Basil was kidnapped from his village on St. Nicholas Day to serve as a cupbearer in the Sultan's palace. After grieving for one year, the parents prayed to St. Nicholas for the safe return of their son. The boy was miraculously whisked away from the court to his home that very day, still wearing servant's clothing.

The crusading Christians did not succeed in their primary mission to permanently rescue Jerusalem from the Moslem infidels. They did, however, manage to draw the Church closer together. But the Holy Wars, which lasted for over two centuries, indirectly effected the future of the Church, Europe, and ultimately the world. While the Church had grown stronger through the unifying goal of the Crusades, the soldiers of the cross were exposed to differing lifestyles as they traveled to foreign lands. Exposure to new ideas most assuredly sparked an eagerness for freedom of thought and adventure outside Roman Christendom. Marco Polo's travels through China no doubt added to this desire for adventure as well.

The Middle Ages produced a Christmas season that, although still pagan in nature, was the merriest of holidays for everyone, with the Church playing a major role in its celebration. Many old superstitious customs and rituals, which had been given Christian translations, were taken to the limits of indulgence. A tightly woven canvas of religious beliefs, winter customs, and revelry reflected the highest point of the Roman Christendom. While this medieval Christmas tapestry was strengthened by the crusading spirit of the Middle Ages, it was, at the same time, made vulnerable to change and new ideas.

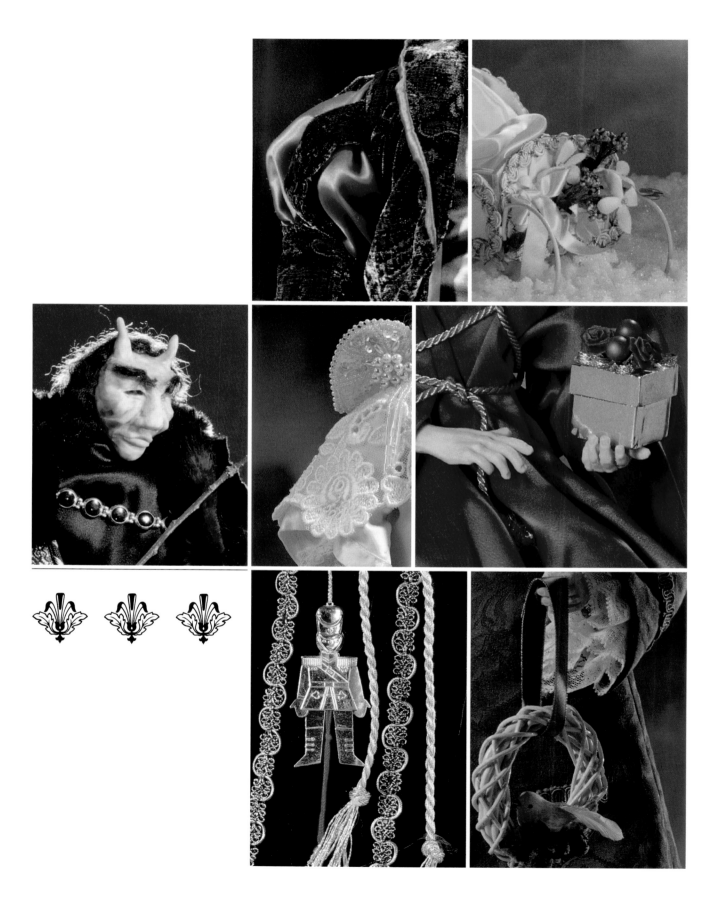

A Season Reformed

The Roman Catholic Church had been at its pinnacle during the Middle Ages and almost all Europeans were required to belong. Possibly because of this mandate, some less than desirable men attained high positions of authority within the Church. These appointments resulted in extensive corruption. Many Christians had become disillusioned with the Church and its Catholic doctrine as the dawning of a new era began to overshadow the Middle Ages.

Although Church corruption was partially to blame, it was not the sole reason for discontentment and rebellion among Christians. The adventures of Marco Polo and the Crusades undoubtedly laid the groundwork for new interests outside the Church, which resulted in the rebirth, or Renaissance, of the arts and sciences. The search for knowledge and understanding in the world of science and philosophy was discouraged by the Church because many thought such learning opposed religious doctrine. Renaissance art still centered around religion and decorated all churches, but artists such as Michelangelo and Leonardo da Vinci added a quality of humanness never before seen.

European contacts with the East came to a halt after the Moslems closed the busy East-West trade routes through Constantinople. Alternate routes to the Orient were sought in an effort to continue the trade for spices, silks, and other luxury items to which the Europeans had become accustomed. It was the relentless quest for an ocean passage to China, along with the scientific invention of the compass, which ultimately led to the historic 1492 voyage of Christopher Columbus and the discovery of the North American continent.

The Church grew less important to many Europeans as interest in the outside world moved to the forefront. The desire for freedom of thought replaced the hold the Catholic Church had had over the people's lives for so long. All the while customs of the Christmas season were being altered as geographical and spiritual changes occurred in Europe. The closely woven threads of the medieval Christmas tapestry began to separate as the pull of reform forced Christians to chose between the old Roman Catholic doctrine and the new patterns of religious beliefs.

While sea captains and their crews were charting perilous voyages across the oceans, religious reformers ventured forth on a rough journey away from the customs and traditions of the Catholic Church. Martin Luther, a German friar, nailed a protest on the door of a church in Wittenberg, Germany, on All Saints' Day, 1517. His protest openly denounced Catholic doctrine and officially marked the beginning of the Protestant Reformation. Luther's intention was not to create a new church but only to reform the old Roman Church. Nevertheless, the Lutheran doctrine quickly spread through the German regions and grew too strong to suppress.

Numerous religious groups broke away from the Roman Catholic Church, and within a short span of twenty years, dozens of Protestant denominations and sects appeared in Europe.

The religious changes which took place in 16th century Europe were met with strong opposition from the Catholic Church. Beliefs which differed from Church doctrine were called heresies, and individuals accused of spreading opposing ideas were severely punished. The Inquisition, originally used to purge Spain of Moslems and Jews in earlier centuries, was re-established to pass judgments on heretics in an effort to protect the integrity of the Church and its principles.

As the main defender of the Catholic faith in Western Europe, Spain led the Counter-Reformation. These efforts were financially supported with the gold and silver acquired from her exploitations in the New World. This vast fortune, along with profitable royal marriages in Europe, made the Spanish Empire most formidable. But neither Spain nor the Inquisition could squelch the rapidly growing number of Protestants. New reform ideas continued to flourish.

Holland became a part of the Spanish Empire in 1555 when its provinces were transferred to Philip II, the Spanish king. At about the same time, Holland was experiencing the undercurrents of religious reform. But the Protestant Movement, which discouraged the celebration of saints' days as being too "popish," had little effect on the Dutch. St. Nicholas was the patron saint of Dutch sailors, and his feast day remained popular even though Calvinism was beginning to take a firm hold in the Northern provinces.

According to Dutch legends, St. Nicholas chained the devil, **Black Peter** (Zwarte Piet), and forced this dark adversary to tote the gifts and birch rods for the St. Nicholas Day celebration. Dutch children half feared Black Peter, who sometimes chased them about with the rods. He kept a record book of good and bad deeds and carried a large sack into which he could stuff naughty little children.

Black Peter was smeared with soot since he was the one who climbed down the chimney with a bag full of toys and rods. He placed a gift in each little wooden shoe left beside the fireplace. The custom of entering a home through the chimney had roots in the old pagan myths of Berchta. Ghostly creatures who flew up and down the chimneys were thought to bring good luck to the household. As a throwback to these yesteryears, today's Santa Claus climbs down the chimney instead of entering through the front door.

Although the Reformation seemed to have no ill effects on the celebration of St. Nicholas's Feast Day in Holland, Black Peter went through a transformation when Dutch independence was finally won from Spain in the 1600's. The saint's helper took on the appearance of a Moorish court page instead of a devil with horns and black cape. Black Peter, the dark skinned part-Moor, part-Spaniard wore short puffed breeches, hose, and a plumed beret. Black Peter's portrayal as a Spanish servant mocked Spain's former dominance and symbolically reassured the Dutch of their new-found freedom.

Black Peter, St. Nicholas' Moorish helper, carried the birch rods, toys, and a little book with a list of the good and bad deeds of each Dutch child.

Knecht Ruprecht was masked as Saint Nicholas' devilish helper.

62

In some regions of Germany, St. Nicholas's devilish helper was **Knecht Ruprecht** who had supposedly been Berchta's bondsman in pagan days. His name even means "Servant Ruprecht." A child's behavior improved at the mention of Knecht Ruprecht's name because his appearance was frightful. He was covered in fur or straw and sometimes even horned like the devil, with fiery eyes and a long red tongue. Promises of good behavior from the children thwarted any punishment that may have been meted out by the scary servant's switches. As the Reformation spread across Northern Germany, Knecht Ruprecht became the alter-ego of St. Nicholas. In some regions he dressed in high boots, white robe, blonde wig, and mask. Although Knecht Ruprecht delivered gifts to the village children, he was more concerned with their prayers and competence in Biblical teachings.

Since ancient times, the birch rod or switch has been a significant part in the role of the gift bearer or his helper, symbolizing both displeasure and the fate of little children.

Old traditions and legends of Knecht Ruprecht still exist in some regions today, but in the weaving of the Christmas tapestry, threads have been rearranged with parts of one story being blended with parts of another. Ironically, in Southern Germany, where the Catholic influence is still strong, Knecht Ruprecht wears the robes of a bishop, while Nicholas (no longer referred to as "saint") sports the red fur-trimmed suit similar to the American Santa Claus. The pair visit the kindergartens and schools to inquire about the children's behavior. On the eve of Nicholas Day, little German children put out their shoes or stockings to be filled with small gifts. The turn-about of characters demonstrates the effects the Reform Movement had on customs and traditions.

Gifts were usually toted in a large sack, sizeable enough to carry away a naughty child.

In an effort to rid the reformed churches of customs thought to be "popish," the St. Nicholas Feast Day was purged, and the Christmas season was modified in the Protestant regions of Europe. Each area created its own gift bearer who delivered presents to children on Christmas Eve instead of December 5, as Catholic tradition had long dictated. In the Alsace region of Germany, the legends of the **Christkindl,** a petite angel messenger, replaced the gift-giving saint. She was dressed in radiant white and wore a jeweled crown. The Christkindl entered the house through a window left unlocked. After placing gifts beneath a little evergreen tree, she would ring a tiny bell. Candles in the windows helped light her way. In the spirit of the Christ Child, candles are still placed in windows today as a sign of welcome. This new figure attributed more emphasis on the birth of Christ without destroying the custom of gift-giving.

In some regions children believed the little Christkindl acted as a Christmas messenger sent from the Holy Child in heaven. Bavarian children thought Nicholas conveyed their requests up to heaven and that it was the Holy Child who actually brought the gifts on Christmas Eve. "Christ bundles" were filled with candies, cakes, toys, caps, scarves, mittens, and useful items such as books, pencils, and paper. The sacks were placed beneath the Christmas tree. Birch rods, called "Christ rods," were attached as a reminder to behave in the coming year.

Various legends of the Christkindl spread from the German border province into France where her name was changed to le Petit Noel (Little Christmas). Whereas the German angel was thought to be a little girl with blond hair, an older boy was chosen to represent Christkindl at the Christmas Mass in France. It wasn't long before the legends of Christkindl were shared by both Protestants and Catholics in Central and Northern Europe.

Like almost all other gift bearers, Christkindl was soon accompanied by an unusual servant known as a Christmas Man. He toted the heavy bag of toys for the small angel, but his main duties centered around discipline. This companion sometimes assumed the combined identities of St. Nicholas and his pagan helper. The saintly character had gone through a metamorphosis as a result of the Reformation. St. Nicholas, the bishop, had exchanged his elegant velvet and satin robes for a fur cape and cap as indicated by the names Ru-Klas (rough Nicholas), Peltznickel (fur-clad Nicholas), Belsnickel (Nicholas with bells), or Aschenklas (Ash Nicholas). Although the Roman Catholic Church condemned these semi-church figures in the 1600's, they remained popular, even among the Catholics.

In Germany's Rhineland after the Reformation, Peltz Nickel accompanied St. Nicholas and Christkindl on surprise visits to every household. The trio's visits began on the first Sunday in December and continued through Christmas Eve. Peltz Nickel rewarded the children if they were able to recite their prayers properly, and each mother was given a switch to be used to discipline her children during the following year. Customs similar to those of Peltz Nickel found their way to America with the German immigrants in later years.

After the Reformation, the tiny Christkindl became the giftbearing messenger in Germany on Christmas Eve.

ngels have always
played a part in the
Christmas season. **The Angel**
represents all of God's messen-
gers who spiritually help and
guide man through his life on
earth. In many regions of the
world, the angel is the gift
bearer of good tidings at
Christmas time.

The Hungarian Angel
brings the Christmas tree. In
Czechoslovakia, children
receive holiday goodies from
an angel dressed in white, who
leads St. Nicholas (Svaty
Mikulas), and his evil-looking
helper, Cert, down a golden
cord from Heaven.

Grouped with angels
are other heavenly gift bearers
such as Poland's Good Stars.
Father Star, accompanied by
the white-robed Mother Star,
distribute presents to those
whose prayers and songs are
recited properly.

Kolyada traveled by sleigh through the deep Russian snow on Christmas Eve.

ussian Christianity had developed through the Greco-Byzantine wisdom, whereas Western Europe had been educated through a Roman-Latin culture. Aside from its Eastern Christian religion, Russia was further separated from the West when its principalities fell to the autocratic rule of the Tartars of Mongolia from the 13th to the 16th century. Due to its isolation, Russia was neither affected by the Renaissance nor the Protestant Revolution which occurred in Western Europe during the same period.

Nevertheless, a parallel can be drawn between the Russian **Kolyada** and the German Christkindl. Kolyada, just like the angel messenger, was depicted as a young girl dressed in a white robe who arrived on Christmas Eve. Kolyada was drawn through the deep snow in a beautiful white sleigh. She was attended by maidens who sang carols as they traveled from house to house. The carolers received gifts in exchange for their melodious tunes.

The "Kolyadki," or carols, passed down through the ages, had their roots in pagan culture. The songs were usually religious in spirit and expressed hope for a plentiful crop. The verses retold the ancient myths of the sun, moon, and stars. Some sources say that Kolyada may have represented the sun goddess of pagan times. Interestingly, the Russian name for the Christmas season is "Kolyada" which comes from Kalendae, or the Roman Calends, the winter festival observed in ancient days.

It was not Martin Luther, but King Henry VIII who was responsible for the demise of the Catholic Church in England during the early 16th century. However, the King's motives were clearly not religious reform. He sought an annulment of his marriage to Catherine of Aragon because she gave him no male heir. The Pope's refusal to grant the annulment angered the willful king who married Anne Boleyn anyway, without consent of the Catholic Church. Henry VIII was promptly excommunicated.

Undaunted, Henry established the Church of England and appointed himself its head. The King never truly opposed the Catholic Church and consequently, organized his Anglican Church with similar doctrine. In doing so, the court preserved the medieval Catholic customs of the Christmas celebration. But the tradition of masking, so popular through the Middle Ages, was curtailed in the streets during the reign of King Henry VIII because of thievery. It became customary, instead, to stage mystery plays at the royal courts. *St. George and the Dragon,* an allegory from a book of saints' lives written by a monk in the 13th century, became the most favored Christmas play. St. George stood for goodness or faith, and the dragon represented wickedness.

The King and his court continued to spend large sums of money on elaborate feasts and entertainment during the Christmas season. The **Spirit of Christmas,** a symbolic figure of good cheer, brought an abundance of special foods, wine, and revelry to the English holiday feast each year. The smiling giant evolved from a combination of Saturn, the ancient Roman god, and the Germanic All-Father god. The celebrations of Saturnalia were transported to Britain during the early centuries of Rome's occupation of the region. Christian missionaries had also found their way to the northern island before the Roman legions abandoned their outposts in the 5th century. With the departure of the soldiers, the partly Romanized, partly Christianized Britons fell prey to pagan warbands of Angles and Saxons who sailed across the North Sea from Northern Germany and Denmark. Subsequently, customs and legends of the Wodan meshed with the celebrations of Saturn. Because the Spirit of Christmas was manifested from the blending of these two pagan gods, he was never really considered a Christian figure.

The white-bearded, towering figure of the Spirit of Christmas wore a crown of holly, ivy, or mistletoe on his head and always carried a large wassailing cup. Dressed in high boots and a fur-trimmed green or scarlet robe, he led a parade of mummers and players through the village streets. As spokesman for the motley group, he stood before the gathering crowds and recited the introduction to the holiday presentation.

The jovial "Spirit of Christmas" symbolized the good cheer during the holidays.

Indulgences of the monarchy were vehemently condemned by the growing number of Puritans who wished to "purify" the Church of England of all Catholic practices. The hardworking Puritans, who wanted to control personal morality, disapproved of the dances, masques, carols, plays, and feasts which accompanied the Christmas celebration. They felt these practices were heathen and not acceptable Christian conduct.

When the Commonwealth, led by Oliver Cromwell, finally gained dominance over England in 1649, Christmas celebrations were abolished by Act of Parliament, including the high-spirited antics of the Lord of Misrule and the carousing Spirit of Christmas. Attempts to enforce the new Puritanical laws caused a ruckus and just added to the reveling behavior. Anglican preachers, resenting the directives of the purifiers, continued to decorate their churches with "pagan" greenery and held services on Christmas Day anyway.

Although the Puritans were in power for only eleven years, their impact was felt for another century. Most customs of celebration were toned down if not altogether forgotten, yet the jovial and robust Spirit of Christmas managed to survive the Puritan ban and later became England's well-known Father Christmas. The custom of role reversal and the Lord of Misrule never again entertained the royal courts since the ruling monarchs were reluctant to turn over their power to anyone, even in jest.

The symbolic figure of **Sir Christmas** was the first seasonal character to emerge after the restoration of the holidays. He was not a religious figure but a rather fashionably dressed gentleman who added a human touch to the season. Sir Christmas was invited into each household to sit by the fire and chat. Neither gift-giving traditions nor disciplinary duties were ever associated with this subdued visitor. The revelries of the medieval feast were lost forever, and to many, Christmas became a rather quiet holiday with simply a good meal, a glass or two of ale, and a friendly game of cards to mark its existence.

The Reformation Movement had its effect upon the design of the Christmas tapestry. The pagan color and subtle religious shadings so long in the making had begun to fade and the frayed and worn threads of the festive Catholic observances were unraveling. The newer strands of Protestant Christmas customs, which were both spiritual and joyful, stood in sharp contrast to the stark Puritan point of view. The Yuletide fibers of Anglican traditions added a social but not a particularly religious element to the cloth. These scattered fragments, many of which had once formed a tightly woven canvas of European Christmas customs, were brought to the New World, and into a new beginning.

Mirrored 5 Traditions

The historic voyage of Christopher Columbus in 1492 was followed by several hundred years of exploration and colonization. Adventurous souls from many kingdoms spread diverse European cultures and Christianity throughout the New World. Each dawning settlement in the land across the sea reflected the religious beliefs, customs, and traditions of its Mother Country.

By the mid-17th century, North America had been divided into three major spheres by the Spanish, French, and British. Explorers and Catholic priests set out together to found New Spain. The Spaniards conquered the Indians of the southwestern regions of North America, and the priests baptized the heathens into the Catholic Christian faith. The new Spanish towns or missions were named after Christian saints. But the Spanish population was scant in the western regions of North America because Spain's interests were concentrated in treasure-rich Central and South America.

The French explored the interior of the new continent and claimed the central lands which extended from Quebec, Canada, south to New Orleans on the Gulf of Mexico. The ruling Catholic monarchs in France never allowed the hated Protestant French Huguenots to settle in the North American territory of New France. Except for the Jesuit priests, who were sent to the wilderness to convert the native Indians to Catholicism, and the fur traders, Frenchmen in New France, like the Spanish in New Spain, were few compared to the numbers of settlers who colonized British possessions on the eastern shores of the New World.

Unlike the Spanish and French spheres, the region from the Atlantic Ocean west to the Appalachian Mountains was settled by many nationalities, each with its own distinct traditions. Although religious customs varied, most of the early settlers on the East coast were Protestant. Virginia reflected customs of the Anglican Church of England, which contrasted with those of Puritan New England. The Dutch and Swedish settlements along the Hudson and Delaware rivers were brought under jurisdiction of the British crown by the mid-1600's.

An open policy employed in colonizing the East accounted for its religious and cultural diversity, as well as its rapid growth to over a million and a half people by the mid-18th century. It was this hodgepodge group of colonists on the Eastern seaboard who banded together to carve out a great nation in the New World with borders stretching west to the Pacific Ocean.

But the "New World" of the colonists was not really so new. It had been home to many Indian tribes for more than ten thousand years. Although appearances and life styles were completely different, Indian religious ceremonies closely paralleled those of the settlers' pagan ancestors. Men from the Hopi tribe of Arizona celebrated a religious winter Bean Dance. Masked and costumed as Kachina spirits, they secretly danced around the blazing Kivas fire for eight days. On the ninth day of the rituals, Nataaska, the Black Ogre spirit, publicly pretended to flail the children who had misbehaved during the year, a custom strikingly similar to that of St. Nicholas's helper. Little wooden Kachina dolls, handpainted in symbolic colors to represent certain spirits, were given as gifts to the Indian children. These and other religious customs and traditions of the American Indian seemed to reinforce the universal threads of beliefs shared by the ancient peoples of Europe.

The Christmas tapestry, worn thin from religious strife which had plagued Western Europe during the 16th and 17th centuries, was brought piecemeal to America. Each colony clung to its own threads of the season. With time, a bond formed among the colonists, and religious differences were set aside. A mending process began to reweave the threads of religious discord until a bright new Christmas tapestry, which included all customs and traditions, took shape.

J̶ust before the Christmas holidays in 1606, three small ships set sail from London across the vast Atlantic Ocean. This voyage carried one hundred and twenty Englishmen who had hopes of making their fortunes in a new land, but they were not prepared for life in this rugged place and barely survived the first few winters. Nevertheless, they managed to build the first permanent English settlement in North America and called it Jamestown.

The region surrounding Jamestown slowly began to develop as English families were enticed to move to the New World by changes in policy that gave the newcomers their own land to farm. Since there was a ready market for tobacco, a plant introduced to Europeans by the Spanish explorers in the 16th century, the colonists cultivated the strange weed. As the tobacco plantations grew larger, the owners became wealthier, and a very comfortable lifestyle developed for the Tidewater planters and their families.

After the fall harvest the Virginia colonials had plenty of time to celebrate the Christmas holidays in Anglican fashion. These customs were observed even during the hardships of the early Jamestown settlers. Captain John Smith and a group of his men celebrated their first Christmas in the New World at the Kecoughtan Indian village. According to records, the friendly Powhatans prepared a feast of oysters, fish, wildfowl, and bread for the holiday feast.

Christmas festivities on the Virginia plantations imitated the elaborate celebrations of merry olde England before the days of the Puritanical Commonwealth. But the hospitable Tidewater planters added a graciousness and warmth of their own to the Christmas season. During the holidays, friends and relatives visited the great manors for weeks at a time. The house guests were entertained with fancy balls, parties, foxhunts, billiards, and cards. In keeping with ancestral tradition, the halls of the elegant mansions were beautifully decorated with evergreens of ivy, holly, rosemary, and mistletoe.

The light of the Yule log's glow flooded the main hall. Plantation slaves were sent into the forests to find the log. Adorned with holly used to kindle the fire, the Yule log was ceremoniously carried into the "big house." It was in the slaves' best interest to find the largest tree available because they were allowed time to pursue their own interests while the Yule log burned.

Christmas feasts on the plantations were almost as lavish as those enjoyed in the royal courts of England. Traditional favorites from the Mother Country were served, but the feast was enhanced by dishes typical to the Virginia region such as turkey, ham, wild game, oysters, and rich fruit cake. A mixture of spices, milk, eggs, and grog, called eggnog, replaced the customary English punch. Much of the savory holiday fare served on the old southern plantations are seasonal favorites even today.

The benevolent gift bearer was not part of the early colonial Christmas celebration. Instead, token gifts were given to servants on St. Stephen's Day, the day after Christmas, and occasionally children received small gifts on New Year's Day. European traditions surrounding St. Nicholas were not observed in Virginia until sometime in the 19th century.

Meanwhile, the settlers in the Northeastern region of America created a lifestyle far different from that of the southern planters. The majority of New England's early population were Puritans who were wealthier and better educated than the Pilgrims who had settled at Plymouth. English charters allowed the Puritans to establish their own form of government and church in the New England colony. Puritans had always disapproved of the seemingly indulgent religious celebrations in the Mother Country, and Christmas in America was no exception. Laws were passed in 1659 prohibiting any observances of the festive season in the colony. For more than one hundred years, until these laws were repealed, New Englanders faced

endlessly cold and dreary winters without the uplifting spirit of the Christmas celebration.

The Dutch settled in New Netherland located between the Puritan North and the Anglican South. They were forced to surrender their claims in the New World to the British in 1664. The important Dutch port of New Amsterdam was renamed New York in honor of the Duke of York to whom the land was granted by the king of England. Parcels of land along the Atlantic seaboard were gradually given to relatives or friends or were, on occasion, used as payment for the king's debts. Generally, each province or colony had its own distinct religious belief which reflected regional customs and traditions brought by the settlers from their homelands. The constant movement from one colony to another helped spread these diverse customs.

The people who settled in Maryland brought Catholic customs to that colony. In 1633, the province of Maryland was granted to a Catholic, Cecil Calvert, the 2nd Lord Baltimore. Many persecuted Catholics found refuge in this colony where freedom of religious consciousness was provided. Consequently, the religious traditions and customs of Maryland were quite different from those of the Puritans in New England or the Anglicans in Virginia.

During the 1800's, Belsnickel was a frightening sight to the children of Pennsylvania and Maryland as he held his whip high above their heads.

ther nationalities influenced the customs and traditions in the English colonies as well. In 1681, William Penn inherited a charter for the region of Pennsylvania, which had been given to his father in payment of the king's debt. Penn, an English Quaker, decided to build a community based on peace and love. His "Holy Experiment" not only attracted Quakers from England, Wales, and Ireland, but appealed to the Scotch-Irish Presbyterians, Swiss and German Protestants, and Jews from all over Europe as well. They eagerly accepted Penn's invitation of religious freedom, representative government, and inexpensive land in the Pennsylvania colony.

The many hollow, sphere-like bells worn by Belsnickel contained a loose ball which jingled with movement. Bells have been a part of secular and religious life, proclaiming glad news since the 6th century.

These groups added more customs and religious beliefs to an already diverse culture within the region. The Germans, in particular, brought many unique customs of the Christmas holidays to America, including the traditions of a menacing creature whose origins go all the way back to the ancient times of Berchta.

Traditions of the German-American **Belsnickel** (Peltznickel) evolved from the customs of the bearded and chain-rattling helper, Peltz Nickel, who accompanied the Christkindl and St. Nicholas in the old country after the Reformation. Dressed in a long, shaggy fur coat and hat, and brandishing a rod or whip, Belsnickel was undoubtedly as frightening a sight to the Protestant and Catholic children of Pennsylvania and Maryland as he was to the little ones in Germany. The noise of his dragging chain, combined with the jingling bells he wore or carried, made eerie sounds. Belsnickel entered through the front door and scattered nuts, cakes, raisins, and sweets on the floor. Fearing lashes from the mysterious figure's whip, the children dared not touch anything before interrogations of their behavior were completed. This scary character was usually a neighborhood friend or relative disguised in a bizarre costume and mask. Eventually, Belsnickel disappeared from the American Christmas festivities when a gentler and kinder figure became more popular.

The term "Belsnickeling" was given to a custom similar to the mumming and wassailing traditions of medieval Europe. The people dressed in strange costumes, went from house to house, and "performed." If no treat was offered for their antics, the group resorted to mischief. The Halloween "trick or treat" customs of the 20th century evolved in part from this tradition.

The customs surrounding Belsnickel or Peltznickel varied somewhat from town to town. Another form of "Belsnickeling" occurred in Pennsylvania on New Year's Day, sometimes called Bel-Schnikel Day. It, too, reflected the old European mumming customs and superstitions.

German nutcrackers, a Christmas favorite among children and adults, are known the world over for their handsome shapes and sizes.

The town's people dressed in costumes and riotously welcomed in the new year. And of course there was noise — guns were fired and bells were rung. A milder version of "Belsnickling" can be seen in the annual Mummer's Parade held in Philadelphia each New Year's Day.

It is believed that German immigrants were also the first to introduce the Christmas tree to America. The German Christmas tree was generally small and was not decorated until Christmas Eve. Old records indicate that evergreens from Germany's Black Forest were sold during Christmas at the marketplace in Strasbourg as early as 1604. The trees were decorated with colorful paper roses, apples, cookies, and gold foil. So legend tells, Luther placed candles on the branches of the evergreen tree because he wanted to recreate the beauty of the moon glistening on the snow-laden trees he had seen while on a walk in the forest. But the Christmas tree's origin as a Christian symbol dates back to an 8th century legend.

One Christmas Eve St. Boniface, an English missionary in Germany, found pagan worshippers about to make a sacrifice to their pagan god. Boniface quickly drew attention away from the gruesome ceremony by cutting down a large oak tree with a single swing of his axe. Impressed by the missionary's unusual strength, the people began to ask questions about the Christian God. Boniface told the pagans to take the small fir, which was hidden behind the giant oak, into their homes. Thus the mighty oak, a symbol of strength to the pagans, was replaced by the small evergreen, the symbol of peace and the everlasting life of Christ.

As ofttimes happened when stories were repeated time and again, the legends of the little Christkindl, transported to America by the Germans, became confused with those of her helper. The Christkindl's delicate image was transformed into a kindly old man with a long white beard and fur-trimmed coat. The small angel messenger disappeared from holiday stories and a newly created **Kriss Kringle** assumed the duties of the Christmas Eve gift bearer, bringing presents and a small tree to children of America. The name was possibly an English mispronunciation of the German word "Christkindl." As the years passed, his legends criss-crossed with others being told, and before long, Kriss Kringle was pulled through the sky in a sleigh by his reindeer. Just like today's Santa, he slipped down the chimney with a bag full of toys for good little boys and girls.

Sometimes the kindly Kriss Kringle left gifts among the branches of the Christmas tree.

By the mid-18th century, many poor immigrants arriving in America found farmland scarce on the Eastern seaboard. In search of a place to grow crops, the Scotch-Irish and German farmers moved to the plentiful lands of the fertile Shenandoah Valley, America's first real frontier. Into the unsettled regions of western Virginia, the settlers carried their own special traditions and customs.

Christmas celebrations in the "up country" surely must have brightened the spirits of the self-reliant frontier families, who endured never-ending hardships in the often hostile territory. So far from the shops of the coastal towns, the holiday became a crafter's event. Toys and decorations were hand-made from materials found on the farms or in the forests. Mittens, scarves, and socks, knitted from spun yarn which had been dyed in bright colors, made very useful gifts. Rag dolls were sewn from scraps of material and corn dollies were fashioned from corn shucks. Painted pinecones, nuts, and gingerbread cookies in a variety of shapes decorated the freshly cut evergreen tree. The children eagerly awaited a visit from the **Frontier Gift Bearer** who came "a-rapp-tap-tapping" on their window panes. Adapting to his new surroundings, the rugged gift bearer probably wrapped himself in buckskin and fur as he toted a burlap sack of whittled toys over the mountains and into the valleys.

The more adventurous pioneer families headed further west across another ridge of mountains into the Ohio Valley, where fighting broke out with the French and the Indians. Unable to halt the expansion of the English colonies, the French were forced to give up New France. Following the French and Indian Wars, the fiercely independent colonists began to challenge British authority. In 1776, the Continental Congress adopted the Declaration of Independence which launched the American colonies into five long and costly years of fighting.

With the surrender of the British at Yorktown, colonial independence was won. A government and Constitution acceptable to "all the people" was of utmost importance. Creating this Constitution was not an easy task. All the diverse cultures, denominations, and social beliefs found within the thirteen colonies, along with the many religious sects that never found acceptance in Europe, had to be considered when the laws of the land were written down. It's not surprising that the Founding Fathers of this great new nation stressed the importance of democracy with the separation of church and state, a concept unheard of in European history at that time.

Children of the rugged American pioneer families anxiously awaited hand-crafted gifts from the Frontier Santa.

Although European influence declined following the Revolution, Americans never totally forgot their roots. An interest in early Dutch heritage was revived in the early 19th century. Dutch settlers who came to New Netherland brought the celebrations of St. Nicholas Day. Little Dutch-American children were soon anticipating the December 6 visit of the austere saint who sailed into the New York harbor on a ship ladened with toys and books from Holland. When the British took over the Dutch settlement in America during the mid-1600's, they were exposed to the Dutch Sinterklaas (St. Nicholas) and may have incorporated his customs into their twelve days of Christmas. It is believed by some that the little English children were fascinated with the customs of their Dutch neighbors and wanted to put out their shoes on December 6th too.

In 1809, Washington Irving wrote the delightfully entertaining satire, *Diedrich Knickerbocker's History of New York from the Beginning of the World to the End of the Dutch Dynasty.* In this mixture of historical facts and old legends, Irving described the old Dutch Sinterklaas as a stocky little man with a jolly manner. He wore Flemish trunk hose instead of the Bishop's ecclesiastical robes, and a broad-brimmed hat replaced the miter. His new appearance possibly reflected a combination of the stern Sinterklaas and the jovial English Father Christmas or Spirit of Christmas which meshed during the 1600's in New York. Irving's **Father Knickerbocker** also smoked a clay pipe and flew over the rooftops in a wagon filled with gifts for the sleeping children. For many American children, Irving's story was their first introduction to the legends of the Dutch Sinterklaas.

On December 6, 1810, the New York Historical Society held its first annual "Celebration of the Festival of St. Nicholas." As the celebration grew over the years, the saint became more popularly known as "Sante Klaas," and by the end of the century he was called "Santa Claus." In 1822, Clement Clark Moore, a professor of Greek and Hebrew in New York, wrote a Christmas poem for his children called "A Visit from St. Nicholas." Twenty-two years passed before the poem appeared in print under the title still well-known as "The Night Before Christmas." Moore's good old St. Nick seemed to combine the characteristics of Washington Irving's stocky little Dutchman, Father Knickerbocker, with the German Kriss Kringle and a bit of personality from the elfish little Scandinavian nisser. Thus, St. Nick became a right jolly olde elf with a long white beard. Dressed in fur from his head to his foot, St. Nick is as dear to us today as he was to Americans in Moore's time.

Christmas became a legal holiday in the United States in 1836. The holiday season reflected a multitude of customs and traditions from many nationalities and Christian faiths, both Protestant and Catholic. Various threads of lively German customs were braided with the festive strands of Christmas cheer celebrated by the English and Dutch. To this composite, colorful hues of French and Spanish traditions were interwoven to form a beautiful all-inclusive American Christmas tapestry.

The Mardi Gras, a celebration known the world over for its masquerades, parades, and

Father Knickerbocker toted a basket filled with toys for the Dutch children of New York.

Thomas Nast's illustration of a Civil War Santa was shown in Harper's Weekly in 1863.

carnival atmosphere, was brought to America by the French. Since 1857, New Orleans, Louisiana, has officially hosted the Catholic festival of Mardi Gras which begins on Twelfth Night and ends just before Lent. The procession was originally a French religious celebration that was incorporated into the mumming parades during medieval Christmas festivities. The custom was ultimately moved to the pre-Lenten celebrations as a prelude to the forty-day Lenten period of fasting and penance in preparation for Easter. The gala festivities took the name Mardi Gras from the fat ox which led the procession. Elaborate floats, costumes, masks, and music are the key elements of today's Mardi Gras celebrations, which are also held in Paris, Rome, Venice, Munich, and other European cities with large Catholic populations.

Just when America was establishing her own identity in the world, contention between the Northern and Southern states began to split the new nation apart. A divisive and costly civil war ensued. At the request of President Abraham Lincoln, Thomas Nast drew an illustration of Santa in a soldier's uniform, which appeared on the cover of Harper's Weekly in 1863. Perhaps it was the President's hope that the "peace and friendship" shared during the holiday season would draw the Union together. But even the patriotic **Civil War Santa** in the fur-trimmed uniform of stars and stripes couldn't deter the fighting which lasted for five long years.

During the 18th and 19th centuries, an unusual type of revolution took place in Europe. Originating in England, the "Industrial Revolution" gradually spread to the European continent and America. Some historians believe the greatest advances in civilization occurred during this period in history due to many new inventions; but at the same time, these accomplishments had a devastating effect on the poor masses.

In the early 1800's, the majority of the English population lived in small country hamlets. Customs and traditions of the Christmas season in the English countryside were poetically expressed by John Clare in "December: Christmas" written in 1827. The houses were thoroughly cleaned and decorated with evergreens and holly boughs. Windows, doors, tables, candlesticks and even pictures on the wall were decked with an artistic eye. Ivy draped the hearth where the Yule log burned, and a slip of mistletoe hung from a beam in the ceiling. The peal of the bells rang out in every village and wassailers sang for "a pence and spicy ale." Mr. Clare described the "Morrice dansers" in gay ribbons who acted out a play and the "clown-turned-King for a penny praise." Gingerbread, sugar plums, merry toasts and special dishes were all a part of the holiday. The little children excitedly awaited the toys brought by the "comers round." Mr. Clare's memories of Christmas are not too unlike our own.

But this quaint lifestyle, with its old customs, was lost to villagers who moved to the cities seeking work in the fast growing industries. The slums and tenement housing of the poor British workers stood in sharp contrast to the beautiful, big Victorian homes built by a rising new middle class.

Christmas observances had all but died out in the crowded city of London where the majority of the population were either too impov-

England's turn-of-the-century gift bearer was inspired by John Tenniel in 1896. His engraving became the most popular visual of the generous gentlemen, lasting for more than twenty-five years. The Tenniel Santa shared similarities with the American Santa Claus. He was a rotund, little character with a long white beard. He wore a red hood and a long red jacket trimmed in white fur. A crown of holly encircled his head just like England's old Spirit of Christmas.

erished or over-worked to celebrate. The deplorable living and working conditions of London's poor inspired Charles Dickens to write his famous masterpiece, *A Christmas Carol,* in 1843. Just as Dickens had intended, his story increased social awareness and compassion in the wealthier Londoners and gave new meaning to the spirit of Christmas. The significantly more religious themes of "alms for the poor" and "good will toward men" were cultivated into the English Christmas celebrations.

Parallel to this literary influence, Prince Albert of Germany introduced Christmas customs of his country to England when he married Queen Victoria. The German holiday was a family celebration focusing on the children. England's **Victorian Father Christmas,** more closely akin to the Christkindl or the American gift bearers, became the children's generous holiday patron. An elegant red, fur-trimmed coat and clay pipe of the Father Christmas replaced the long green robe, wreath of holly, and wassailing cup of the old Spirit of Christmas.

The German Christmas tree became the highlight of the English holidays. Queen Victoria and the royal family's Christmas celebrations, centering around home and hearth, set an example for almost every English household. Traditionally, the German tree was small and presents were nestled among its branches. In adapting the tree to the English Christmas, gifts were placed below a massive tree that had been beautifully decorated with many candles and ornaments.

Old customs, banned as too pagan by the Puritans' standards, were given a special new place in the Victorian celebrations. Evergreen decorations were first displayed by the pagans to honor the supernatural spirits and deities believed to dwell in all waters, mountains, groves, and pastures. After conversion to Christianity in the Middle Ages, evergreens were braided into wreaths which symbolized the circle of God's love with neither a beginning nor an end.

Caroling was another old tradition which gained popularity during the Victorian era. The French word "carole" meant a circle dance of many people accompanied by song. Carols were handed down from generation to generation. After years of Christian influence, pagan carols became associated with Christmas celebrations. Strolling groups of minstrels and caroling children were popular throughout the Middle Ages. Even though caroling was forbidden by law, along with all other Christmas customs deemed too heathen in the 1600's, the ancient songs managed to survive in the small villages away from the watchful eye of the Puritanical government. These songs found new life as caroling became a cherished part of the English holidays. Many traditions of the old-fashioned Victorian Christmas are just as popular in America today as they were in England over one hundred years ago.

*The hobbyhorse, baby doll,
and building blocks were
favorite gifts from the
Victorian Father Christmas.*

America, too, felt the consequences of the Industrial Revolution. As the 19th century drew to a close, Europeans sought job opportunities in this land of opportunity. Millions of anxious immigrants from Italy, Hungary, Czechoslovakia, Poland, and Russia entered America's large cites on the Eastern seaboard. These newcomers represented the last major influx of European cultures to America and introduced an array of unique customs and traditions from the Eastern Orthodox and Roman Catholic celebrations of their homelands. Their customs lent a more religious quality to the ever-changing holiday season. This new spiritual emphasis may have been the inspiration for Henry van Dyke's story, "The Other Wise Man." Henry van Dyke (1852-1933) was an American clergyman, educator, and author who composed this beautiful new Christmas legend of giving, caring, loving, and sharing.

According to the story, **The Other Wise Man** set out alone on the long journey to Bethlehem to present the newborn King with precious gifts — a leather purse filled with gold coins that he had saved over the years, a beautiful blanket of many colors in which his mother had woven the story of his tribe, and a pearl of great value.

Not far into his journey, the fourth Wise Man encountered a poor soul who had been injured and left to die in the hot desert. Using his gold as payment for treatment of the man's wounds, the Wise Man continued on his way. Once again his trip was delayed when he saw an old woman crouched outside the massive gates of a walled city. The doors had been closed at sundown and would not open again until the following morning in order to protect the city's inhabitants from the treacheries of roaming thieves and murderers. The elderly woman was forced to spend the night huddled against the stone wall in the frigid night air. Realizing she was in danger of freezing to death, the Wise Man unhesitatingly gave his treasured blanket to the grateful woman and journeyed on. Nearing the end of his travels, the fourth Wise Man met a young maiden whose life was being threatened because of her father's unpaid debts. The Wise Man kindly offered his pearl, the last of his intended gifts, as payment for the father's obligations.

Upon reaching Bethlehem, the fourth Wise Man told the sad stories of the people he had encountered on his journey. The Wise Man had come such a long way to worship the newborn King but, sorrowfully, had no gifts left to offer. To his surprise, the Wise Man was commended for his acts of generosity and kindness. By giving his only gold, warm blanket, and precious pearl to those in need, The Other Wise Man had given the greatest and most beautiful gift of all — the gift of love.

The Other Wise Man humbly gave the most important gift of all — the gift of love.

ach nationality settling in America contributed its own distinctive threads to the Christmas tapestry. But of all the holiday traditions, the universal favorite is the custom of gift giving. Children everywhere have anxiously anticipated the visit from a magical gift-bearing figure for more that two thousand years.

Many whimsical illustrations of jolly old **Santa Claus,** appearing in American books throughout the 1800's, depicted a chubby little man with a jolly manner and long white beard. These pictures were inspired by the writings of Moore and Irving who had compiled bits and pieces of old European myths, lore, and legends to create the characteristics of the American gift bearer. Odin and Berchta rode through the night sky during Yuletide on a white horse, while Santa makes his rounds on Christmas Eve in a sleigh pulled through the sky by reindeer. The reindeer's names of Dancer and Prancer have their roots in Norse mythology. Even Santa's entry into every home through the chimney has its origin in old pagan myths.

And Santa, who checks his list twice for those who are naughty and nice, is following in the footsteps of Black Peter who carried a book of childrens' names for the same purpose. Black Peter carried the sack of gifts for St. Nicholas; now Santa Claus totes his own bag overflowing with toys made in the North Pole workshop by busy little elves who look quite similar to the Scandinavian Julenisse.

Stockings hanging by the fireplace are filled by Santa just like the three maidens' stockings were filled by the kindly Nicholas, Bishop of Myra. Santa's jolly disposition is most likely inherited from England's fun-loving Spirit of Christmas or Father Christmas. The American Santa Claus, without a doubt, resulted from a combination of the many legendary figures who have brightened the lives of children down through the ages.

Thomas Nast's first Santa Claus sketch, which appeared in 1863 in *Harper's Weekly,* was followed by many delightful illustrations of the American gift bearer each Christmas for over twenty years. It doesn't matter what name is used: Santa Claus, St. Nicholas, or Father Christmas; Thomas Nast's popular drawings transformed St. Nicholas into the Santa Claus we know today.

ur Christmas tapestry is indeed a cherished treasure reflecting the histories, legends, and traditions of many people. The almost two-thousand-year-old threads of early Christian traditions woven with strands of ancient pagan customs formed the heart of the Christmas tapestry. It began to unravel during the Reformation, but in time, a larger, more beautiful design was created. An understanding of the historical events which occurred through the ages, coupled with the mind-set of the people who created and shaped this tapestry, provides us with an explanation of the holiday's universal appeal and the special place a gift bearer has in the design. We, too, will pass on the old traditions, in addition to newly created customs of our own, to future generations as the threads of the Christmas tapestry continue their intricate weave into the twenty-first century.

Artist's Note

Many people have asked me how I started making Christmas figures. Well, a friend suggested I try making Victorian Santas since she thought, as an artist, I'd enjoy it. She and a neighbor taught me the basic steps in creating a figure. I was truly excited about the process, especially the sculpting, although stories of "exploding clay" in a kiln scared me. I experimented with a clay medium called Sculpey, which could be baked in the oven. It was much easier to handle, and definitely the choice for me.

An old photograph of my Dad was the inspiration for my first figure. His round face, high cheek bones, receding hair line, and cleft chin were carefully sculpted into the clay. Since then I have created many faces. In trying to capture a realistic quality in each, I've referred to pictures found in magazines and books or from the more familiar faces of family members and friends. A true love for sculpting developed.

These figures were not just sculpted. Each had to be individually assembled. Wire was twisted into an armature and covered with a "bodysuit" of muslin, which was then stuffed with polyester. At first I was not interested in this part of the project, and it showed. But the oddly shaped bodies were hidden under long and flowing fur-trimmed robes. Many hours were spent experimenting with various wire gauges to find the strongest yet most flexible; a variety of wooden or metal dowels were attached to bases in search of the best minimal visual support.

At the same time, I bought or collected small toys to fill the Santas' sacks and assorted

fabrics, furs, jewelry, and other unusual items to enhance the dolls. But, other than their unique faces, each figure seemed the same. I wanted to create one-of-a-kind characters. To find uncommon Christmas figures, I borrowed a friend's book on various gift givers. This book was the first of many I read that opened a whole new world of Christmas customs.

Setting aside initial plans "to make and sell Victorian Santas," I began a search for other Christmas characters who had enhanced the traditions of the holiday through the centuries. Each new figure created represented a particular tradition or legend, time period, or culture.

After reading a wonderful little book called *Doll Making, One Artist's Approach* by Robert McKinley, I disassembled the original

twenty-eight figures. I saved the heads, discarded the bodies and most of the costumes, and started all over again, paying closer attention to the entire figure. The dolls began to show movement. Each new costume was designed with greater detail and accuracy.

Through making these sculptures came the desire to create a visual history showing our ties to the past. The thirty-seven Christmas dolls which were linked together by the threads of historical events, religion, and customs needed a written explanation. Additional research and determination led to the development of a manuscript. From this work the book took shape and form, much like my characters.

The figures depicted in this book are only a representation of the many Christmas characters who exist in legend and the customs which surround them. They are my interpretive blending of historical and religious facts and the lore of two thousand years. Through on-going research, I continue to discover new characters and a rich tradition of customs, but they are too numerous to include.

Artist . . . Brenda Morris earned a B.F.A. in Fashion Illustration and Advertising from Virginia Commonwealth University in Richmond. Her twenty-six year artistic career includes more than 10 years as a free-lance graphics designer. A native of Richmond, she lived in Germany for two years. Brenda has a love of travel and a fascination with history, and she has combined these two interests with several trips through Europe. Brenda lives in Richmond with her husband and their two children, all of whom share her love of seeing the world.

Editor . . . Lynne Robertson received her B.A. in Journalism and M.A. in English from the University of Richmond, Virginia. She has twenty-five years career experience in journalism and advertising including 10 years as Copy Director for a retail corporation. A Richmonder, Lynne's passion for travel has taken her on trips throughout the continental United States and Canada, as well as Europe, England, Scotland, Russia, New Zealand, Australia, and Hawaii. Lynne is currently a free-lance writer and editor based in the Richmond area.

Photographer . . . Jeff Saxman is a graduate of the Rochester Institute of Technology in Rochester, New York. He has won awards for his photography in both Rochester and Richmond, Virginia, where he currently works on tabletop, editorial, and stock photography. He has spent time, as well, working and teaching in the woods of Maine. Originally from Pennsylvania, Jeff moved to Richmond in 1990, where he presently lives with his wife and young son.

Educators . . . Ceilia Donohue and Nancy Payne, through their teaching experience and first-hand knowledge of differing cultures, were able to check the manuscript for accuracy of facts and historical interpretation. Ceil relied on her graduate studies in political science, medieval history, theology, and church history in her proofreading effort. Nancy has a master's degree in Education. Both women are avid travelers, and between them, they have seen the world from Europe, Russia, and China to the Land Down Under.

1 The Roman *is properly dressed in a satin-lined white wool toga and purple leather sandals trimmed in gold. He carries typical seasonal gifts — a candle, wreath, and clay doll. His face is sculpted in the likeness of my brother.*

2 The King of Saturnalia, *in a multi-colored satin toga over a loose-fitting tunic, holds a pair of dice in one hand, and in the other he clutches a lantern to ward off evil spirits. He wears a pointed hat, a symbol of importance, and his leather sandals are purple, signifying royalty.*

3, 4, and 5 The Magi *are bedecked in gowns of satin, mantles of velvet or silk, and leather sandals. The purple and black satins were salvaged from my daughter's prom dresses.* **Melchoir's** *velvet coffer is an earring box adorned with a filigree and stone broach;* **Gaspar's** *myrrh is represented by an old perfume bottle;* **Balthazar** *holds an antique carved wooden jar. Each costume is enhanced with sequined trim, stones, feathers or jewelry, some of which were found in antique stores or flea markets.*

6 St. Nicholas, the Bishop of Myra *wears a silk skirt beneath the satin and lace frock. His cape and slippers are made of rich velvet. The mother-of-pearl necklace was found in an antique store, but the silver and pearl cross pendant was a Christmas gift from my Dad many years ago.*

7 St. Lucia *is crowned in a wreath of greenery and candles. Rosette trim enhances her dress of antique lace. The velvet cape and shoes are decorated with handcrafted satin roses. Lucia holds a lucykatter bun in her outstretched hand. In olden days an "X" with curled ends, symbolic of a cat, was placed on top of each bun. The markings were intended to chase away evil spirits in very superstitious times.*

8 Kolyada *is wrapped in an off-white paisley brocade fabric trimmed in white mink. The fur was salvaged from an old suit collar my daughter found in a Vermont antique store. Her boots are fashioned from old kid gloves. The opal clasp is a discard from my mother-in-law.*

9 Odin *sports a tunic of black and silver threads created from an evening gown belonging to my mom. The black fur cape was cut from a coat found in an antique store. The pouch is leather and decorated in an antique trim and earring. The wool boots are held in place with leather strappings. His shield is fashioned from thin metal which was rubbed across a design on the back of a glass plate; the center is an antique button. His face is sculpted in the likeness of my husband.*

10 Berchta *sits hunched on a gnarly wood stump in a black satin gown; her cape is taffeta outlined in floral tapestry trim. She holds a "crystal ball" — an antique marble made to glow by the photographer's skillful lighting technique. Berchta's right foot is unusually large as it is her treadle foot when spinning. The porcelain doll in billowy chiffon represents the souls of children left in Berchta's loving care.*

11 Holda *is draped in a cape of white feathers, each glued into place on heavy felt. Antique cloth hat flowers hold the goddess' golden hair in place and fill her wicker basket.*

12 King Wenceslas *wears a royal blue velvet robe bound in white fur marked to look like ermine. His blue satin tunic covers a silk dress. The crown was made from metal pressed into shape and decorated with stones and trims; his leather-soled boots are made of white felt.*

13 Kolya *is clothed in a heavy white wool coat and hat, each edged in mink cut from an old full-length fur. The coat is held together with tiny gold chains cut from a necklace. His rust colored underskirt is made of heavy satin saved from the lining of the mink coat. Antique velvet holly berries trim his hat.*

27	28	29	30	31	32	33	34	35	36	37
Sir Christmas	*The Angel*	*Kriss Kringle*	*Belsnickel*	*The Frontier Santa*	*Father Knickerbocker*	*The Civil War Santa*	*Victorian Father Christmas*	*The Tenniel Santa*	*The Other Wise Man*	*Santa Claus*

26 The Spirit of Christmas *wears a coat made from green velvet fabric I purchased over twenty years ago while living in Germany. The wassail cup is wooden; the suede boots are bordered in mink. This figure's face was sculpted in the likeness of my Dad.*

27 Sir Christmas *dons a straight, collarless brocade coat with pearl buttons taken from an old necklace. His hat is sewn from felt, stiffened into shape and trimmed with antique velvet flowers and leaves. The playing cards in his hand were found among my daughter's old toys.*

28 The Angel *is dressed in a gown of burgundy satin. Her wings are made from feathers, each individually glued to a buckram frame. The crocheted blanket in the cradle was recently brought back from Croatia by a good friend.*

29 Kriss Kringle *wears a silk-lined velvet coat bordered in mink and red rosettes. His dress is silk brocade. The suede toy sack and boots are made from a jacket found at a second-hand store.*

30 Belsnickel *is an intimidating figure to little Pennsylvania Dutch children. His full-length mink coat and hat, trimmed in many small bells, jingle as he moves about from house to house. His baggy knickers are wool. The handle of his whip is made from a button taken off an 1890's velvet coat.*

31 The Frontier Santa *totes a burlap sack of toys and gifts for the "up country" children. His suede jacket, pants, and boots are fashioned from a flea market purchase and trimmed in mink. An old purse strap now serves as the Santa's belt; its buckle was a wooden earring. The powder horn which hangs around his neck is just an odd-shaped bone button.*

32 Father Knickerbocker *carries his basket of toys to the children of New York dressed in a cape of velvet dating to the 1890's; his slouch boots are remnants of a suede coat*

from a second-hand store; the laced vest is the satin lining of an old coat; the hat is constructed of heavy leather. The wooden toy windmill, house, and animal were bought at the United Nations building in New York City many years ago.

33 The Civil War Santa *sits atop a gold drum (a flower planter turned upside-down) in a blue cashmere jacket with gold stars. His white satin breeches are stitched with red satin ribbons. The tasseled hat and leather boots are edged in mink.*

34 The Victorian Father Christmas *wears a fashionable mink-trimmed, red velvet coat and black satin pants. The hobby horse he clutches in his hand was used as a department store Christmas decoration years ago. The doll and the block were among my daughter's outgrown toys.*

35 The Tenniel Santa *sits astride a Yule log in a velvet knee-length coat and footed trousers held in place with leather strapping. His head is covered in a hooded short cape.*

36 The Other Wise Man *kneels in homage to the Infant King. His robe is green taffeta; the fringed blanket around his shoulders was made from a fashion scarf. The pearl he holds comes from a broken necklace; the leather purse is made from scraps of leather and trimmed with braiding. The jewel on his turban is an antique earring once belonging to my mother-in-law.*

37 Santa Claus *is dressed in the traditional red velvet suit and floppy pointed hat, both bound in the familiar white fur. His wide, black leather belt is fastened with an old belt buckle. His boots are black velvet trimmed in fur. Santa's needlepoint stocking is one I stitched years ago; his pipe is sculpted from clay.*

14	15	16	17	18	19	20	21	22	23	24	25	26
The Asian	The Morris Dancer	The Mari Lwyd	The Medieval St. Nicholas	Befana	Baboushka	The Lord of Misrule	St. Francis	Christkindl	Black Peter	Knecht Ruprecht	Julenisse	The Spirit of Christmas

14 The Asian *is sculpted from a picture in* National Geographic. *His velvet coat is trimmed in mink and gold-threaded ribbon. The yellow satin brocade dress was cut from an Oriental outfit found at a second-hand store, and the little dolls in the velvet sack are taken from a pin cushion bought in San Francisco's China Town. His unusual antique necklace shows a picture of warriors on one side and an Oriental design on the other.*

15 The Morris Dancer *is decorated in satin ribbon streamers and bells. The fez is hardened felt with a chiffon veil attached. The tambourine, leather leg band, and satin boots jingled as he danced about the festive crowd.*

16 The Mari Lwyd *is covered in a white wool blanket embellished with glass beads taken from an antique necklace. Multi-colored ribbons decorate the carved wooden horse's head. Her mane is made with hair clipped from my old chignon dating from the 1960's. Hidden beneath the blanket is a small figure in brown wool who worked the horse's wired jaws.*

17 The Medieval St. Nicholas *is cloaked in red wool piped with brown mink and a dagged liripipe hood; his boots are green leather. He holds a small German ornament. The little hand-carved wooden figure in his leather sack was purchased in Berlin in the early 1970's. His cane was cut from a small tree limb; the spirals were formed from vines which had grown around the limb.*

18 Befana *is stooped from toting a large sack of toys and bundle of switches on her back. She wears a black velvet, smocked and hooded cape enhanced with colorful Florentine trim befitting the old Italian gift bearer. Her dress is black satin with burgundy cuffs and collar.*

19 Baboushka *wears a cape of brown velvet cut from an 1890's garment. Her apron was made from pieces of an antique table scarf. Tucked in the pocket is an authentic Russian stacking doll given to my daughter by a close friend of mine. The little horse in her basket is an old German Christmas ornament.*

20 The Lord of Misrule *struts about in platform shoes which have extremely long toes held up by a cord that fastens just below the knee, a fashion in medieval Europe. He wears satin puffed pants with ribbon trim and his sleeves are sequined. A cat's head, ribbons, and bells adorn his staff.*

21 St. Francis *is sculpted from an old picture of my great-grandfather. His habit is made of brown wool with maroon lining; the sandals are fashioned from leather strips cut from an old belt. The sculpted infant is placed in a manger made of sticks and filled with straw.*

22 Christkindl *stands barefoot in a white satin dress with a lace top cut from the collar of a sweater belonging to my daughter. Antique lace trim edges the gown's hem. The angel messenger's wings are made from sequined applique; the crown is a Christmas ornament embellished with additional stones.*

23 Black Peter *is attired in a velvet, puffed-sleeve jacket lined with antique purple; the teal satin vest is fastened with antique buttons; his shoes are of purple suede. He carries a leather-bound book tied together with black satin ribbon.*

24 Knecht Ruprecht *looks ominous in a black fur cape clasped with an old onyx watch band. His black satin gown is decorated in gold trim. This horned, devilish-looking character carries a birch rod and rattles his chain to frighten the children.*

25 Julenisse, *almost invisible as he sits among the scattered straw and toys, smiles as he eats the hot porridge left in a giant lacquered bowl with his brightly hand-painted spoon. He is dressed in velvet britches held up by ribbon suspenders. The little nisse's unusually long pointed cap and equally long white beard touch his lap.*

Resources

A Christmas Testament. Arranged and introd. Philip Kopper. New York: Stewart, Tabori & Chang, Publishers, Inc., 1982.

Abrams, Richard I., and Warner A. Hutchinson. **An Illustrated Life of Jesus, from the National Gallery of Art Collection.** New York: Bell Publishing Company, 1988.

The Annotated Christmas Carol, A Christmas Carol. by Charles Dickens. Introd., notes and biog. by Michael Patrick Hearn. New York: Avenel Books, 1976.

Babushka, an old Russian Folktale. Retold and illus. Charles Mikolaycak. New York: Holiday House, 1984.

The Book of Christmas Carols. Secaucus: Chartwell Books, Inc., 1985.

Branson, Branley Allan. "Kachina-Free Spirits of the Hopi Indians." **Early American Life,** Feb. 1975, pp. 20-22 and p. 62.

Brinton, Crane, John B. Christopher, and Robert Lee Wolff. **A History of Civilization.** 2 vols. Englewood Cliffs: Prentice-Hall, Inc., 1955.

Chalmers, Irena, and friends. **The Great American Christmas Almanac, A Complete Compendium of Facts, Fancies, and Traditions.** Gen. Ed. Carlotta Kerwin. n.p. Viking Studio Books, 1988.

Christmas Tales for Reading Aloud. Comp. and adapted Robert Lohan. 1946; enl. ed. New York: Stephen Daye Press, 1966.

Christmas Treasures, A Keepsake Collection for the Holidays. Editorial research Barbara Louts and Aileene Neighbors. Kansas City: Hallmark Cards, Inc., 1976.

Clapham, Frances M., ed. **Picture History of the World.** New York: Grosset & Dunlap, 1986.

Coffin, Tristram Potter. **The Illustrated Book of Christmas Folklore.** New York: The Seabury Press, 1973.

Davison, Michael Worth, ed. **Everyday Life Through the Ages.** London: Reader's Digest Assn. Limited, 1992.

Del Re, Gerard, and Patricia Del Re. **The Christmas Almanack.** Garden City: Doubleday & Company, Inc., 1979.

Doten, Hazel R., and Constance Boulard. **Fashion Drawing, How To Do It.** 1939; rev. ed. New York: Harper & Row, Publishers, 1953.

Ebon, Martin. **Saint Nicholas, Life and Legend.** New York: Harper & Row, 1975.

Engle, Paul. **An Old Fashioned Christmas.** Illus. Eleanor Pownall Simmons. New York: The Dial Press, 1964.

Flaum, Eric. **Discovery Exploration Through the Centuries.** New York: Gallery Books, 1990.

Foley, Daniel J. **Christmas the World Over, How the Season of Joy and Goodwill Is Observed and Enjoyed By Peoples Here and Everywhere.** Radnor: Chilton Book Company, 1963.

Giblin, James Cross. **The Truth About Santa Claus.** New York: Thomas Y. Crowell, 1985.

The Glory and Pageantry of Christmas. Eds. Time-Life Books. Special Ed. Maplewood: Hammond Incorporated, 1963.

Grolier Encyclopedia, Vols 1 - 20. 1960.

Hadfield, Miles, and John Hadfield. **The Twelve Days of Christmas.** Boston: Little, Brown and Company, 1961.

Hottes, Alfred Carl. **1001 Christmas Facts and Fancies.** Illus. Lindsay Lockerby Field. New York: A.T. De La Mare Company, Inc., 1946.

Jones, E. Willis. **The Santa Claus Book.** New York: Walder and Company, 1976.

Kainen, Ruth Cole. **America's Christmas Heritage.** New York: Funk & Wagnalls, 1969.

Kelley, Emily. **Christmas Around the World.** Minneapolis: Carolrhoda Books, 1986.

Lawhead, Alice Slaikeu. **The Christmas Book.** Westchester: Crossway Books, 1985.

Lehane, Brendan, and eds. of Time-Life Books. **The Book of Christmas, The Enchanted World.** Alexandria: Time-Life Books, 1986.

Lewicki, Lillian. **The Golden Book of Christmas Tales, Legends from Many Lands.** Painted by James Lewicki. New York: Simon and Schuster, 1956.

Miall, Antony, and Peter Mial. **The Victorian Christmas Book.** New York: Pantheon Books, 1978.

Muir, Frank. **Christmas Customs and Traditions.** New York: Taplinger Publishing Company, 1977.

Papa, Joan Springer. "Der Belsnickel." **Early American Life,** Dec. 1975, pp. 72-75.

Pringle, Mary P., and Clara A. Urann. **Yule-tide in Many Lands.** Illus. L.J. Brigman. Boston: Lothrop, Lee & Shepard Co., 1916.

Richards Topical Encyclopedia. Eds. Ernest Hunter Wright and Mary Heritage Wright. Vols. 1 - 13. New York: The Richards Company, Inc., 1959.

The St. Nicholas Book, A Celebration of Christmas Past. Ed. and introd. Martin Grief. New York: Main Street/Universe Books, 1976.

Sansom, William. **A Book of Christmas.** New York: McGraw-Hill Book Company, 1968.

Spicer, Dorothy Gladys. **46 Days of Christmas.** New York: Coward, MaCann & Geoghegan, Inc., 1961.

Stevens, Patricia Bunning. **Merry Christmas! A History of the Holiday.** New York: Macmillan Publishing Co., Inc., 1979.

The Story of Befana, an Italian Christmas Tale. Illus. and retold Ilse Plume. Boston: David R. Godine, Publisher, Inc., 1981.

The Trees of Christmas. Comp. Edna Metcalfe, New York: Abingdon Press, 1969.

Weiser, Francis X. **The Christmas Book.** New York: Harcourt, Brace & World, Inc., 1952.

Wenborn, Neil. **The U.S.A., A Chronicle in Pictures.** New York: SMITHMARK Publishers Inc., 1991.

Wernecke, Herbert H. **Christmas Customs Around the World.** Philadelphia: The Westminister Press, n.d.

The Whole Christmas Catalogue. Tucson: HPBooks, Inc., 1986.

Willson, Robina Beckles. **Merry Christmas, Children at Christmastime Around the World.** Illus. Satomi Ichikawa. New York: Philomel Books, 1983.